THE TRUE ISRAEL OF GOD

RUSSELL MERCER

MID:AMERICA
Bible College

Printed in the United States of America
International Standard Book Number: 1-883928-21-4
Library of Congress Catalog Card Number: 97-070782

Unless otherwise noted, all Scripture quotations are from the
King James Version of the bible. Personal emphasis, noted by
italics, has also been added in various verses.

Published by:
Mid-America Bible College
3500 S.W. 119th Street
Oklahoma City, Oklahoma 73170
405-691-3800

Table of Contents

Acknowledgments

There are so many I would like to mention who have been helpful to me. Even as I try, I know I will miss a number of people who have inspired me in the writing of this book. To you I say your influence and encouragement have been vital and I thank *each one.* of you.

I thank Dr. John Conley for his support and help in making my "script" what it is. The love, friendship and fellowship that we have long shared could only come through being of the same "family." It's the love of God that is in each of our hearts.

I thank Donna Conrad, my pastor's wife, for the help she has given me in the initial typing of my script.

I thank Dr. Forrest Robinson, my friend of many years and a close companion in my work for Mid-America Bible College. His spirit of love has been with me through many years, and it took a lot of something special to always get along with me! He has it, and I am so very grateful. For your remarks about my book, Dr. Robinson, I say a very loud "Thank you!"

Special thanks go to my dear brother Earl Shaffer. Even from the time he was just a young boy, we have had a great love one for the other. He has conducted revival meetings for me and I for him through the years. His comments on my book are greatly appreciated. He is one of the best preachers I have ever heard.

I want to thank my own publishing house, Warner Press, Anderson, Indiana, Vital Christianity, the publishing board of the Church of God, and its members for the use of songs, script, etc.

Preface

I feel very much like Luke felt as he started. "Forasmuch as many have taken in hand to set forth in order a declaration of those things which are most surely believed among us, even as they delivered them unto us, which from the beginning were eyewitnesses, and ministers of the word; it seemed good to me also, having had perfect understanding of all things from the very first, to write unto thee in order, most excellent Theophilus, that thou mightest know the certainty of those things, wherein thou hast been instructed" (Luke 1:1–4). It seemed good to me also.

When so many have written much on the topic of this book, you might question, Why another? I cannot say for sure just when I decided to write a book on this subject, but I have been making notes for several years. I think perhaps it has been my in-depth study of the Messiah in Jewish and Christian apocalypses that spurred me on to write this book.

I have availed myself of all the helps and commentaries within my reach, as well as all that I have listed in my bibliography. I have not known any other writer on this subject. It seems to me this study pictures all the false teaching of our age; however, it brings out bright the eternal Savior of man and the complete plan of redemption for mankind. For me, it is heart-rending to picture the Jewish apocalypses.

I must confess that after fifty-eight years in the ministry, I have made thousands of notes, some or many gained from the sayings of others. Wherever this has happened in my writing, I gladly give the credit due, as much as my memory allows.

The height of my dream and prayer for this book is that it might be used as a textbook for studies at midweek prayer meetings, Sunday school classes, sermons, and of course individual studies.

Russell W. Mercer

THE TRUE ISRAEL OF GOD

Chapter 1

THE IDENTIFICATION OF THE MESSIAH IN JEWISH AND CHRISTIAN APOCALYPSES

*T*he *True Israel of God* is a doctrinal book with a new approach. Several years ago, when everybody was writing choruses, I asked God to let me write a chorus. He did just that, and not just one, but four! One that I have used in revival meetings all around the states and Canada has been this one. (This chorus is so good to get people to raise their hands in testimony.)

Have You Started for Heaven?
Have you started for heaven, dear friend, tonight?
Do you know the sweet peace of the Lord?
Do you know that He is dwelling down deep in your heart?
Have you started for heaven tonight?
Yes, I've started for heaven, dear friend, tonight!

Yes, I know the sweet peace of the Lord.
Yes, I know that He is dwelling down deep in my heart,
Yes, I've started for heaven tonight!

In this study I am not trying to cover all the Jewish and Christian apocalypses, only those that deal, to a degree at least, with the Messiah. Many of the texts that deal with this subject are corrupt, so I am showing you what appears to be the Messiah in the first four chapters of this book. I will try to present each scripture that relates to the Messiah, as well as a brief summary at the end of each chapter or book and a more complete summary at the end of Chapter 4.

Daniel

Daniel, being the oldest (about 165 b.c.) of the Jewish apocalypses known, will be dealt with first.

Daniel 2:45 — "Forasmuch as thou sawest that a stone was cut out of the mountain without hands." This undoubtedly had reference to Christ and Church; use it either way.

Daniel 2:44 — "God of Heaven shall set up a kingdom." Christ is undoubtedly included in this picture.

Daniel 3:25 — "King sees four men — one like unto son of God." Some people have thought this to be Christ. Critics seem to think this is an angel. I like to think this was my Lord and Savior, Jesus Christ.

Daniel 8:25 — "And through his policy [probably the Roman government or kingdom] also he shall cause craft to prosper in his hand: and he shall magnify himself in his heart, and by peace [margin says prosperity] shall destroy many: he shall also stand up against prince of princes: but he shall be broken without hand."

Daniel 9:24 — Daniel prays to know when seventy weeks of captivity will be ended, "and to anoint the most holy." This

10

doubtless has reference to Christ, perhaps as anointed one, prophet, priest and king of all mankind. Also Adam Clark thinks this might include anointing for death.

Daniel 9:25 — "From going forth of commandment to Messiah."

Daniel 9:26 — "And after threescore and two weeks shall Messiah be cut off."

Daniel 10:5, 6 — "Then I lifted up my eyes and looked, and behold a certain man clothed in linen, whose loins were girded with fine gold of Uphaz." "His body also was like the beryl, and his face as the appearance of lightning, and his eyes as lamps of fire, and his arms and his feet like in color to polished brass, and the voice of his word like the voice of a multitude." Compare this with Revelation 1:13, 15. "And in the midst of the seven candlesticks one like unto the Son of man, clothed with a garment down to the foot, and girt about the paps with a golden girdle. And his feet like unto fine brass, as if they burned in a furnace; and his voice as the sound of many waters."

Summary of Chapter

It appears that Daniel sees the future coming of the Messiah, "stone cut out without hands," a king to rule his people. He shall reign for ever and ever. This could hardly be a literal reign as Daniel 8:25 pictures the *Roman government standing against him* — "but He shall be broken without hand." This would show Christ does not use literal force, so hence a spiritual King. Time is marked by his birth—Christ. Christ is picture as anointed King of kings — possibly anointed for death; He is not to reign forever literally but will die and then reign for ever and ever over his people.

Enoch (About 120 b.c.)

Enoch 24:1, 6 and 25:1, 5 gives an account of the tree of life.

This seems to be Christ. "Here is pictured seven mountains. One in the middle is like unto throne of God. He shall come to visit the earth with goodness, but at the day of judgment He will take vengeance on those who do not serve Him. The fruits of this tree of life shall be food to the elect."

Chapter 38 stresses the judgment of the wicked and high people of the earth. They shall not be able to behold the face of the holy, evidently meaning Christ.

Chapter 39. Enoch saw visions of righteous with Christ. "Holy, holy, holy." All elect are to be raised to dwell with Christ.

Chapter 41:9 speaks about God, dividing good from bad, and a judge appointed (this judge the Messiah). "The word that I have spoken, the same shall judge him in the last day" (John 12:48).

Chapter 46:1, 3 — "With head of days — one whose countenance had appearance of man. Face full of graciousness, like holy angels, righteous. He revealeth all the treasures of that which is hidden. Lord of spirits has chosen him." From here on it seems Daniel has been drawn upon. Also this book is sealed for future generations. God shall raise up a king and mighty from their thrones. He shall break the teeth of sinners and put down kings because they do not extol him.

Chapter 48 — Picture Christ as being chosen before, or existing before, the foundation of the world, a fountain of righteousness, *a light unto the Gentiles. In His name they are saved.*

Chapters 49 and 50 mention the Elect One, nothing hid from him. He had glory, majesty, wisdom, and power, and the wicked shall perish.

Chapter 51 — Christ is all powerful — hard metals shall melt away under His power, metal meaning future kingdoms, not His kingdom.

Chapter 53 — Those who abide in Him have rest and peace. The wicked shall be wiped from the earth.

Chapter 56 — All mighty kings and rulers will have to behold the elect one on his throne. Angels shall stir up the Parthians and Medes, and they shall try to tread underfoot the land of the elect. But they shall end up fighting each other. God's people shall survive.

Chapter 61 — The Elect One is long-suffering. All shall bless him on earth and in heaven. None shall perish who trust in him.

Chapter 62 — The kings and mighty are ordered to recognize the Elect One on his throne. One day they will, but they will be terrified; pain shall seize them when they see the Son of Man on his throne. From the beginning the Son of Man was hidden; he was preserved for the elect only. The elect shall dwell with him forever, eat with him, and be clothed with garments that shall not grow old.

Chapter 63 — The mighty shall look upon the Son of Man in shame and shall be driven from him. (A loving God to the elect, but no mercy on the wicked.)

Chapter 69 — Previous to this goes back to Noah, pictures judgment, and then shows the Son of Man appearing to judge and rule.

Chapter 71 — Enoch is taken to heaven and sees the son of Man with God and is told that God never forsakes him. He is everlasting. All shall walk after Him.

Chapter 90 — A white bull was born with large horns. Horns are a symbol of power. Vision just being finished here from beginning to Christ's time. Now transformed into a lamb. His followers become like him with unending life. They return to the state of Eden. Adam was the white bull.

Chapter 92 — *Righteous One* shall *arise* from *sleep and give his* followers power.

Chapter 96 — Look forward, ye righteous, to his lordship — or Christ.

Chapter 99:10 — "Blessed are those who accept and

13

observe the path of the most high. They shall be saved, but woe to those who do not."

Chapter 100:3 — "And the horse shall walk up to his breast in the blood of sinners." This compares with Revelation 14:20 where it says, "And the winepress was trodden without the city, and there came out blood from the winepress, even unto the bridles of the horses, as far as a thousand and six hundred furlongs."

Chapter 100:4 — The Most High will arise to execute judgment.

Chapter 101 — The righteous fear the Most High but not the sinners.

Chapter 105 — I and my son will be united forever with the righteous children.

Summary of Enoch

Enoch pictures Christ as the tree of life, from which comes food to feed the elect. The works of the world shall be tried by Christ. He shall destroy the wicked and cleanse the earth for the elect ones. He is to be a light unto the Gentiles. In his name they are saved. He has glory, majesty, wisdom and power. The wicked will be in terror when they see him on his *throne to judge.* Christ is everlasting, a loving God to the righteous but woe to the wicked.

Chapter 92 — Christ is to arise from sleep and give his followers power.

Enoch sees Christ as literally destroying all the wicked with rivers of blood running over the face of the earth. Just by sweeping His mighty arms to and fro, He will mow down all who ever oppressed Israel! This belief could come from such scenes as when Christ fed the five thousand with five barley loaves and a couple of small fish, when He commanded the roaring sea to be still and many other miracles. They could well see with this kind of King they would never have to fight another battle.

II Esdras

Esdras, as said by some, had this vision shortly after Israel's time of captivity and the rebuilding of the temple (536 b.c.).

Chapter 2, page 42 — "O ye nations that hear and understand and look for your shepherd, he shall give you everlasting rest. For he is nigh at hand that shall come in the end of the world." Just before this speaking about them rejecting him, he mentions a passage about gathering her brood as doth a hen.

Esdras saw upon Mount Zion a great multitude. These were supposed to be ones who have put off the mortal clothing and put on the immortal and have *confessed* the *name of God*. A tall man was putting crowns upon their heads. When Esdras asked who the tall man was, the angel said he was the Son of God.

Chapter 4 — In a vision Esdras asks the angel about the future of the people. The angel told him to listen to a voice. "Behold there was a voice that spake, and the sound of it was like the sound of many waters [many people]." This voice said that after certain things were done Zion would be fulfilled. And when the seal shall be set upon the world that is to pass away, then will I show these tokens: The books shall be opened, etc.

Chapter 7 — The angel tells Esdras: After certain things shall come to pass, the bride shall appear, which has been withdrawn from the earth, and Jesus shall be revealed, and after seven days (the word seven is a symbol of a period of time), the bad shall be destroyed. Good shall be raised up. Then Christ shall be revealed upon the throne.

Chapter 9 — After certain things that I have shown you come, then is the *very time when the Most High* shall visit the earth. The *Most High* is mentioned three times in this chapter.

Chapter 10 — While in a flower garden eating nothing but

15

flowers, waiting on God, he saw a woman weeping for her son. This apparently was the Church and Jesus Christ.

Chapter 11 —The Most High is mentioned three times, speaking of eagles and heads.

Chapter 12 — The Most High is mentioned five times. It's hard to decide whether Christ is meant part of the time. Signs of the second coming are mentioned — this would lead one to believe he is speaking of Christ. The latter part of the chapter says, "And the Lion whom thou sawest rising up out of the wood and roaring and speaking to the eagle and rebuking her for her unrighteousness and all her words which thou hast heard — this is the anointed one whom the Most High hath kept unto the end."

Chapter 13 — (Another dream) The wind came up from the sea (sea symbolic of people). Out of the clouds came the likeness of man. The angel tells him this is the Son of Man. He held neither spear nor instrument of war and slew without literal arms. This son will taunt the people to their face with torments and destroy them. *Most High* is mentioned three times here, probably referring to the Messiah. Again Esdras asked the meaning of man coming up out of the sea. He says no man upon earth can see my son but in the time of his day.

Summary

In this book it appears the author sees a Christ that has already been to earth once.

Chapter 7 — Bride shall appear, which has been withdrawn from the earth.

Chapter 12 — Show me a sign of the second coming.

Chapter 10 — Christ is pictured as having great love for His church to the extent that He is weeping over her.

Chapter 13 — When he comes again he shall destroy all wicked, but apparently *without* weapons of a carnal nature (Daniel 8:25 same picture) and then be their King and ruler.

II Baruch

A Different Picture of the Messiah

II Baruch 29:4 — "And it shall come to pass when all is accomplished that was to come to pass in those parts, that the Messiah shall begin to be revealed." This seems to be mystical — maybe already born but not known.

II Baruch 30:1 — "And it shall come to pass after these things, when the time of the advent of the Messiah is fulfilled, that he shall return in glory."

II Baruch 39:7 — Previous to this speaks of the first to fourth kingdoms that will arise. This sounds like Daniel. Then the Messiah will be revealed.

II Baruch 40:1 — He will sit as a judge to convict and put to death the wicked. a savior for the righteous (literal rule).

Chapter 53 starts a vision (verses 1–12). Where it mentions black water it means the travail of the Messiah. Lightning on the cloud refers to the Messiah.

II Baruch 70:9. Whosoever of the victors gets safe out of and escapes all these things will be delivered into the hands of my servant the Messiah (probably an interpolation — the wicked will be destroyed by Christ).

II Baruch 72:2, 3 — After the Messiah comes all nations that have ruled over Israel in any way shall be destroyed.

Chapter 73 — (After he does this) then peace and healing shall come down. Disease shall withdraw, gladness shall be over the whole earth, wild beasts shall come from the forest and minister unto men. Asps and dragons shall submit to babies.

Summary

We see the Messiah here as living and also dying with his people. The Messiah is a great warrior who slays all of Israel's enemies with his bare hands. In the *Assumption of Moses,*

17

Chapter 10, we find the same picture. It appears that all who are not the chosen will be annihilated.

The Sibylline Books

Book 3:286 — The God of Heaven shall send a king. Each shall be judged with blood and fire. Some think this to be Cyrus — sounds much like Messiah.

Book 3:652-657 — And then from the *sunrise* God shall send a king who shall give every hand relief from the bone of war. Some he shall slay and to others he shall consecrate faithful vows. This shall be done through obedience to God, not just Christ's will. People of God shall be laden with wealth, gold, silver and purple adornment!

Gook 3:741, 742 — But when the fated day shall reach this consummation there shall come to mortals the judgment of the eternal God. All of God's people shall have the best. Earth shall produce without effort. Cities shall be full of good things and fields rich. No more sword of battle, no war or drought, no famine or hail —a great peace throughout the earth.

Book 3:761 — He shall burn with fire the race of stubborn men.

Book 5:256 — An exalted man to come from sky, whose hands they nailed to a fruitful tree; who one day shall cause the sun to stand still. Compare with Luke 23:43, 44 — "And Jesus said unto him, Verily I say unto thee, today shalt thou be with me in paradise. And it was about the sixth hour, and there was darkness over all the earth until the ninth hour."

Book 5:363, 384 — And there shall come from the end of the earth a *matricide*. He shall ruin all the earth and gain all power, but then there will be infinite peace.

Book 5:414, 433 — For there has come from the plains of heaven a blessed man, who has dominion over all. He restored all the wealth which former men took. He burnt up the evil but built the city of God as a jewel of the world, thinking in terms of a literal kingdom.

Summary

It appears to me here that Christ will save those who obey him, and they shall receive great riches. No more aches or pains come to the righteous, but woe comes to the wicked. One who was nailed to the cross shall come and wipe out the wicked and evil — then there will be infinite peace.

IV EZRA

IV Ezra 6:26 — Whosoever shall have survived all these things that I have foretold shall be saved and shall see my salvation and the end of the world. (The reference here seems to be to Christ, a warrior who shall come and slaughter the wicked.)

IV Ezra 7:27, 28 — Whosoever is delivered from the predicted evils, the same shall see my wonders. For my son, the Messiah, shall be revealed. He shall rejoice with the survivors four hundred years, then he shall die.

IV Ezra 9:9 — Survivors and signs before Christ's coming are mentioned.

IV Ezra 12:31, 34 — The Lion spoken of here refers to the Messiah, whom the Most High has kept unto the end, the seed of David. Note Revelation 5:5: "And one of the elders saith unto me, Weep not: behold, the Lion of the tribe of Judah, the Root of David, hath prevailed to open the book, and to loose the seven seals thereof." Here he is identified as one who will reprove and rebuke for their ungodliness; then he shall destroy the wicked (Christ as a literal ruler).

IV Ezra 13:25 — Thou didst see a man coming up from the heart of the sea (The sea is symbolic of people.). This is the *pre-existent* Messiah. He will deliver his creation (the righteous only).

Verse 33 — God tells him this is his Son in the midst of great turmoil.

Verse 37 — He shall stand upon mountain he built, cut out without hands (probably taken from Daniel).

Verses 38, 39 — He shall be made manifest to all men, to reprove the wicked and rebuke them, like unto a storm. Tortures are compared to flames.

Summary

The Messiah is pictured here as one who will torture and then slaughter the wicked, a terrible picture of a bloodthirsty warrior. While the righteous sit around with folded arms, He, Christ, will slay the wicked. The righteous he will save *to be their ruler* .

Ezekiel

The Christ of Calvary

Ezekiel 24:23 — (He has been telling them about a false shepherd who did not take care of the flock.) "I will set up one shepherd over them, and he shall feed them. Even my servant David he shall feed them, and he shall be their shepherd." This is definitely figurative language — trees of the field shall bear fruit, etc. Killing is more of a judging between sheep and goats, good and bad.

Ezekiel 36:26 — "A new heart also will I give you."

Ezekiel 37:24 — My servant David shall be king over them. These spirit-filled dead bones shall be resurrected. Note the valley of "dry bones." Can these live? Ezekiel 37:14 — "And shall put my spirit in you, and ye shall live, and I shall place you in your own land; then shall ye know that I the Lord have spoken it, and performed it, saith the Lord." One shepherd — David, my servant, shall be their prince forever.

Summary

Here we see a different picture. The Messiah here is one with great love. He will feed and nurture his own. He will not slaughter and torture but be a just judge. He will give those who meet his requirements a new heart and place his spirit within them. Even though they are dead in trespasses and sins they can be made alive in the Messiah, and Christ will be their King of kings and Lord of lords forever.

Zechariah

Zechariah 9:9, 11 — "Behold thy king cometh unto thee. He is just and having salvation, lowly and riding upon an ass, even upon a colt, the foal of an ass. The bow shall be cut off. Peace shall come to all nations, and his dominion shall be from sea to sea and from the river to the ends of the earth."

Summary

This would be hard to believe of a literal king. Any literal king would have ridden on a horse, but this was a meek and lowly king who would bring salvation to the world by the shedding of his blood.

The Shepherd of Hermas

Vision 2:19 — "For the Lord hath sworn by his Son, that whoso denieth his Son and him, being afraid of his life, he will also deny him in the world that is to come."

Vision 20 — "But those who shall never deny him, he will of his exceeding great mercy be favorable unto them."

It is my opinion that this book should be in the Canon.

Commands of Hermas, or II Book of Hermas

In the introductory material of this book, while Hermas was praying, a man appeared unto him in the habit of a shepherd, clothed with a white cloak, having his bag upon his back, and his staff in his hand, and saluted him. In asking who he is, Hermas is told, "That shepherd to whose care you are delivered." While he was speaking his shape was changed and then Hermas said, "I knew it was he to whom I was committed." It is this same person who speaks to Hermas through twelve chapters called *The Commands*. Whoever this person is, or if it be Christ, he is teaching or trying to show Hermas:

Chapter 1: Faith in God
Chapter 2: Simplicity and Love of One's Neighbor
Chapter 3: Truth
Chapter 4: Chastity
Chapter 5: Patience and Mercy
Chapter 6: Good and Evil Angels
Chapter 7: The Fear of God
Chapter 8: Self-Restraint
Chapter 9: Trust in God
Chapter 10: Sadness and Joy
Chapter 11: False Prophets
Chapter 12: Combat with Evil Desires

II Hermas 5:10 — "For all such as have repented have been justified by the most holy messenger who is a minister of salvation." The messenger is spoken of again in Chapter 5:40. Similitude — as of giving strength. I have doubt in my mind whether this is Messiah.

The Book of Hermas of Similitudes

The aforementioned shepherd is mentioned in the fifth chapter. He is using parables similar to ones Christ used.

Verse 27 — He is represented to be with Hermas and all who will follow Him.

Verse 41 — He is represented as showing all things unto Hermas.

Verse 46 — In a parable God's Son is the Holy Spirit; also, the servant is the Son of God.

Verse 47 — He represents the Son as giving commands.

Verse 49 — The Son is represented as a servant to man.

Verse 50 — He is represented not as a servant, but as a great power and authority.

Verse 51 — The Son is pictured as suffering so he might blot out the offenses of his own that the father gave him. Contrast with 7:11; He must suffer first, and then God might be moved to forgive.

Verse 52 — He is pictured as a lawgiver.

Verse 53 — He is pictured as all-powerful.

Verse 56 — The Son is pictured as one whom God counsels with. Corrupt text through here.

9:1 —The spirit who told Hermas about church, or a figure of the church in the first part of Hermas, is said here to be the "Son of God."

Verse 4 — Hermas is pictured as unable to understand all the things of the past, but angels have strengthened him. This angel said to be the spirit of the Son of God.

Verse 109 — *The rock and gate to this structure* is the Son of God. This is speaking of a tower that was being built.

Verse 110 — *Christ is very ancient insomuch* that He was in counsel with His father at the creation of all things.

Verse 111 — *He is represented to have* appeared in the last

23

time.

Verse 113 — *No man is to enter the kingdom* of God *unless he take upon him the name of the Son of God.*

Verse 117 — But *no man* shall go to God, but by his Son.

Verse 199 — The Son of God is pictured as tall with angels on his right and left, walking back and forth through the tower, which is symbolic of the church. No angel comes to God but through the Son.

Verse 122 — The Son of Man is pictured as giving power to his followers. Without this they cannot bear his name.

Verse 147 — The Son of God is pictured as having Gospels and his ministry preaching it.

Verse 152 —The Son of God has the power to seal for heaven his own who die.

Verse 154 — The Son of Man seals those who are buried in water baptism.

Verse 166 — The Son of God is for all nations.

Verse 176 — *The Son of God is to rejoice when all the church of God comes under one faith and understanding.*

Verse 235 — "Those who have suffered death for the name of the Son of God shall have their offenses blotted out."

Verse 259 —This verse also mentions deliverance from sin. It appears as though he was speaking about spiritual life.

Summary

This book pictures the Son of God as very ancient — present from the beginning. Nowhere does it mention Christ but uses the term Son of God. The Son of Man is represented as having a church, he being the door, and only through him can man enter. He is represented as having ministers who preach his gospel (9:147). He is to have appeared in the last days. This probably has reference to the first advent of Christ. He is supposed to have suffered so he might blot out the offenses of his own. In contrast to this, 9:154 and other verses show that man is forgiven of sin through baptism. There is no atonement mentioned, yet he promised to give his followers power over sin. He is pictured to be for all nations (9:166; 9:176). *He is to rejoice when all his church comes under one faith, understanding, love, and fellowship.*

The Lost Gospel According to Peter

Peter 1:1 — Christ is before Pilate.

Verse 2 — Christ is about to be crucified.

Verse 3 — He is apparently destroyed of all honor as we watch them drag Him and then spit upon Him.

Verse 4 — On his cross they wrote "This is the king of Israel." By one of the malefactors, who was crucified by his side, he is said to be the savior of men.

Verse 5 — He cried out, "My power, my power, thou has forsaken me."

Verse 6 — When he was laid on the earth, it quaked.

Verse 10 — Even though soldiers kept guard, the Savior arose a conqueror of the grave.

Verse 11 — The soldiers declare to Pilate, "Truly he was the Son of God." Pilate also says, "I am pure from the blood of the Son of God."

Verse 13 — An angel in the tomb declares to Mary, "The Lord is risen and gone whence he was sent."

Summary

In this book Christ is said to be the King of Israel by his enemies, a savior of men by one who suffered by his side. In verse 5 Christ lets us know there is one greater than He, yet He Himself conquered death and the grave. In contrast with other books, He ascended the same day as He arose from the grave.

The Revelation of John

Revelation 1:1 — This the revelation of Jesus Christ.

Revelation 1:2 — Witness of the word of God and the testimony of Jesus Christ. This makes the book Christian and identifies the Messiah as having been here, which the Jews didn't expect.

Revelation 1:5 — Christ is the instigator of these letters, a faithful witness, the first-born of the dead, and ruler of the kings of the earth. By his blood we are saved. He made us to be priests, which gave us access to him.

Revelation 1:7 — Christ shall return; all shall see Him. It pictures Christ as omnipresent, omniscient, and omnipotent.

Revelation 1:13 — In the midst of candlesticks is one like unto the Son of Man. Here Christ is ever near His church, as near to one as the other.

Revelation 1:18 — He is a resurrected Lord, now alive for evermore. He has power over death and hell and is more powerful than the Jews ever thought Him to be, greater than any God they imagined who would "mow down" all who oppressed them.

Revelation 2:7 — The Messiah is identified as a Christ with outstretched arms to whomsoever will serve Him or call upon Him but to those who will not, sudden destruction.

Revelation 2:10 — He is pictured a Christ who can give a crown of life — eternal life — to His followers. There is also no hurt of the second death.

Revelation 2:16 — To those who do not repent, he shall make war (spiritual war) against them. But to those who do, Christ will feed them with hidden manna and give them a new name.

Revelation 2:18 — A Christ who has eyes like a flame of fire, and feet like unto burnished brass.

Revelation 2:26 — A Christ who can give authority to whomsoever he will. He identifies Himself as shortly to come again.

Revelation 3:3 — One who will come as a thief in the night.

Revelation 3:5 — As one who keeps books on his followers or his children, and intercedes with his father for their needs.

Revelation 3:8 — He alone has keys to heaven.

Revelation 3:9. He looks upon all men with love, not just the Jews as they thought and think today.

Revelation 3:11 — Again he warns, I come quickly.

Revelation 3:14 — Once more he is mentioned as the faithful and true witness, the beginning of the creation of God.

Revelation 3:16 — A Christ who will not accept half-hearted worshipers. A Christ who is rich beyond world possessions.

Revelation 3:19 — A loving yet just God reproves and chastens.

Revelation 3:20 — A Christ who stands at the door and knocks, even to the sinner, the one who is lost. A Christ who will sup with his children.

Revelation 3:21 — A Christ who will let those who have overcome sit with him on his throne.

Revelation 5:5 — The Lion who is of the tribe of Judah, the root of David, hath overcome to open the books and seven seals — Christ.

Revelation 5:6 — A lamb, as though it had been slain, with seven horns. Horns are symbolic of power. Christ is seen here as a lamb with great power, the only one capable of opening the book.

Revelation 5:8 — Heavenly beings worship him (symbolic language).

Revelation 5:9 — Slain that he might purchase unto God with his blood, men of every tribe, tongue, people, and nation. It is here that the literal Jew becomes a spiritual Jew in the act of

27

the new birth. As Paul said to one group, "They are not all Jews who say they are. All Israel will be saved." This is spiritual Israel that will be saved.

Revelation 5:12 — The lamb is worthy of this honor.

Revelation 5:13 — Every created thing was heard giving blessing to him.

Revelation 6:1 — The Lamb, or Christ, opens the seals.

Revelation 6:9 — A Christ whom his followers love so deeply they suffer martyrdom as a witness of him.

Revelation 6:17 — Pictures evil forces of the world trying to hide from the wrath of the lamb.

Revelation 7:9 — A great multitude before the lamb, clothed in white robes, indicating they have been washed in his blood. They serve him. *He is their king*. They shall hunger no more, neither thirst. The lamb shall lead, guide, and water them.

Revelation 11:15 — Christ is represented as having a kingdom that belongs to him, the kingdom of the world, and he rules forever and ever. This is both spiritual and literal.

Revelation 12:10, 12 — Pictures Christ as having authority over evil powers. His people overcome through his shed blood.

Revelation 13:8 — The Lamb, who has been slain, who keeps the book of life, knows all his people and they know him, too. All others worship the beast.

Revelation 14:1 — The Lamb is pictured on Mount Zion before 144,000 (twelve tribes of children of Israel, 12,000 each, symbolic of all Israel) who had his name on their foreheads. He is pictured here again as knowing his own; he would see that none were lost.

Revelation 14:14 — Probably the Messiah, pictured at the final judgment as harvesting the earth.

Revelation 15:3 — Pictures those that are saved singing songs of praise to the Messiah. Christ brings his children to safety.

Revelation 17:6 — Again the Messiah is represented as

having people love him so much they die to uphold his truths and doctrines.

Revelation 17:14 — Christ is Lord of lords and King of kings. Evil shall war against him, spiritually, but he shall overcome and his with him.

Revelation 18:25 — Pictures Christ as one who will not always strive with man.

Revelation 19:8 — We see the bridegroom with his bride (Christ and his church); he owns her. All who are invited to the marriage supper are blessed.

Revelation 19:16 — All his followers who have his mark recognize him as King of kings and Lord of lords.

Revelation 20:4 — Christ has all those who suffer with him and for him reign with him.

Revelation 20:11 — Christ is the judge of the world: All shall come forth, the wicked shall be cast in the lake of fire, and the righteous shall reign with him forever.

Revelation 21:2 — Pictures Christ as ready for his bride. And all that overcome shall dwell with him and his Father in their mansion, or our mansion, prepared for the righteous.

Revelation 21:27 — Only those whose names are in the Lamb's Book of Life shall dwell there.

Revelation 22:1 — Pictures the Lamb having the water of life flowing from him.

Revelation 22:3 — The Lord shall permit them to look upon his face. And they shall dwell forever and ever with him.

Revelation 22:16 — I, Jesus, have sent mine angel to testify unto you these things.

Revelation 22:20 — I come quickly.

Summary

We have here in Revelation a beautiful picture of the Messiah. We see that he was offered as a sacrifice so men could be freed from sin. He is different from what the Jews and others

29

thought; he was not to be a literal king, but he was King of kings and Lord of lords, a just judge of both good and evil, far surpassing a literal king, having power over death and hell. He is always near each one of his people or followers. He loves them and nurtures them. He is ever present in time of need. He forever is pleading our case before his Father. Even though we might have to suffer a little here on earth, it will only be for a short time; then we will be with him forever. A celestial home is prepared for his children. He warns us several times to watch, to be prepared; he will come quickly.

A Complete Summary and Comparison of Certain Parts

The Messiah is pre-existent in IV Ezra. The Shepherd of Hermas says "very ancient or from the beginning." The books of the Bible I use, either directly or indirectly, teach a pre-existent Son of God. The other books I use here either do not mention it at all or are very mystical about any pre-existent Messiah.

As we know, and as is plainly shown, the Jewish apocalypses do not recognize the Messiah as having come even though time was changed at his first advent, but the Christian Apocalypses do. II Esdras, Shepherd of Hermas, Lost Gospel of Peter, and Revelation recognize the Messiah as having come to earth already.

Enoch appears to teach a Messiah who literally mows the wicked down: "Rivers of blood shall flow over the face of the earth."

In contrast to this, Ezekiel pictures the Messiah as having great love for his own. He will feed and nurture his own. He is a just judge who will not torture anyone; rather, to the darkest sinner who will come and seek forgiveness he will give a new heart and a new spirit. He is a loving and kind savior of man.

The Sibylline Books picture the Messiah as one who will come and wipe out all the evil forces of the world literally; then there will be peace. In contrast to this, Zechariah shows the Messiah is a meek and lowly king but not of this world, one who will bring salvation to a lost world — every tribe, tongue, and nation. All may be saved if they but accept the Messiah.

In II Baruch the Messiah is pictured as a great warrior who will reach out with his bare hands and destroy all the wicked while the righteous sit back with folded arms.

In contract to this we observe the Lost Gospel of Peter and II Esdras. In Peter we see the Messiah upon the cross of Calvary, with his nail-pierced hands, suffering for the sins of the world, so that whosoever would believe upon him would not perish but have everlasting life. In Esdras he is pictured as having so great a love for his church that he is weeping over her. The wicked are to be destroyed but not through any literal battle.

IV Ezra pictures a bloodthirsty warrior who will unmercifully torture and slay the wicked when he comes to earth, a tyrant who will reach out with a long sword and slaughter any and all who have ever had anything to do with his people Israel; this is a Messiah who has no mercy or love for anyone but his own, and after all are destroyed he will be king of his own.

In contrast to this I take Revelation. John sees the Messiah not as a bloodthirsty warrior but as a Christ who gave his life for the souls of man, as standing and knocking at the heart door, even of those who took his own life. He is a resurrected Lord, King of kings and Lord of lords with power that surpasses even the imagination of those who thought he would rule by literal force. He is represented as having power to open the graves. Needless to say he would only have to speak the word and the wicked would be annihilated. He would not need to resort to literal arms as they thought. He is said to love and nurture his own and to have a heavenly mansion prepared for those who have been faithful unto death.

Let us be faithful and gain that mansion.

Israel and the Kingdom

These are guidelines for interpretation of the Scriptures: "No question can ever be answered scripturally if regard be had only chiefly to what one or two indeterminate texts can be made to teach. . . . It must be answered and those texts explained in keeping with what is plainly the general trend and spirit of the entire body of Scripture teaching on the subject" (G.P. Tasker). "In the interpretation of Scripture it is important to explain the doubtful by the certain. That is, interpret the figurative and symbolical passages of Scripture by the plain and clearly expressed passages. Obscure passages and those hard to be understood should always be interpreted in harmony with plain and straightforward passages elsewhere" (C.E. Brown).

We need to understand that all Bible promises are *conditional.*

Ezekiel 33:12–13 — "Therefore, thou son of man, say unto the children of thy people. The righteousness of the righteous shall not deliver him in the day of his transgression: as for the wickedness of the wicked, he shall not fall thereby in the day that he turneth from his wickedness; neither shall the righteous be able to live for his righteousness in the day that he sinneth. When I shall say to the righteous, that he shall surely live; if he trust to his own righteousness, and commit iniquity, all his righteousness shall not be remembered, but for his iniquity that he hath committed, he shall die for it."

James 1:17 — "Every good gift and every perfect gift is from above, and cometh down from the Father of lights, with whom is no variableness, neither shadow of turning."

Genesis 6:6 — "And it repented the Lord that he had made man on the earth, and it grieved him at his heart."

Jeremiah 18:9–10 — "And at what instant I shall speak concerning a nation, and concerning a kingdom, to build and to plant it, if it do evil in my sight, that it obey not my voice, *then I will repent* of the good, wherewith I said I would benefit them."

Exodus 29:9 — "And thou shalt gird them with girdles, Aaron and his sons, and put the bonnets on them: and the priest's office shall be theirs *for a perpetual statute*."

I Samuel 2:30 — "I said indeed that thy house, and the house of thy father, should walk before me forever: but now the Lord saith, Be it far from me; for them that honor me I will honor, and they that despise me shall be lightly esteemed."

II Samuel 7:10 — "Moreover I will appoint a place for my people Israel, and will plant them, that they may dwell in a place of their own, and move no more: neither shall the children of wickedness afflict them any more, as before time." God promised David that Israel would *move no more*. And yet in 722 b.c. the ten tribes were carried into captivity.

Hebrews 8:9 — "Because they continued not in my covenant, and I regarded them not, saith the Lord."

Abraham was promised all the land of Canaan. "Arise, walk through the land in the length of it and in the breadth of it; for I will give it unto thee" (Genesis 13:17). And yet in Acts 7:5 we read, "And he [God] gave him none inheritance in it, no, not so much as to set his foot on." And if we read Hebrews 11:10 we see the reason why. "For he looked for a city which hath foundations, whose builder and maker is God." The throne was promised to David and his seed forever.

I Chronicles 22:10–13 — "He shall build a house for my name; and he shall be my son, and I will be his father; and I will establish the throne of his kingdom over Israel for ever. Now, my son, the Lord be with thee; and prosper thou, and build the house of the Lord thy God, as he hath said of thee. Only the Lord give thee wisdom and understanding, and give thee charge concerning Israel, that thou mayest keep the law of the Lord thy God. Then shalt thou prosper, if thou takest heed to fulfill the statutes and judgments which the Lord charged Moses with concerning Israel: be strong, and of good courage; dread not, nor be dismayed."

I Chronicles 28:79 — "Moreover I will establish his kingdom for ever, if he be constant to do my commandments and my judgments, as at this day. Now therefore, in the sight of all Israel the congregation of the Lord, and in the audience of our God, keep and seek for all the commandments of the Lord your God: that ye may possess this good land, and leave it for an inheritance for your children after you for ever. And thou, Solomon my son, know thou the God of thy father, and serve him with a perfect heart and with a willing mind; for the Lord searcheth all hearts, and understandeth all the imaginations of the thoughts; if thou seek him, he will be found of thee; but if thou forsake him, he will cast thee off for ever." The condition: "If thy children will keep my covenant and my testimony that I shall teach them, their children shall also sit upon thy throne forevermore" (Psalm 132:12).

God promised the priesthood to the sons of Aaron forever. Exodus 28:1, 43 — "And take thou unto thee Aaron thy brother, and his sons with him, from among the children of Israel, that he may minister unto me in the priest's office, even Aaron, Nadab and Abihu, Eleazar and Ithamar, Aaron's sons. And they shall be upon Aaron, and upon his sons, when they come in unto the tabernacle of the congregation, or when they come near unto the altar to minister in the holy place; that they bear not iniquity, and die: it shall be a statute for ever unto him and his seed after him."

Leviticus 10:2 — "And there went out fire from the Lord, and devoured them, and they died before the Lord."

Genesis 12:3 — God's covenant with Abraham: "In thee shall all families of the earth be blessed."

Acts 3:25–26 — "For David speaketh concerning him, I foresaw the Lord always before my face; for he is on my right hand, that I should not be moved; therefore did my heart rejoice, and my tongue was glad; moreover also my flesh shall rest in hope." Christians are the fulfillment of this promise.

What Is Israel?

The name Israel began with Jacob. "And he said, Thy name shall be called no more Jacob, but Israel: for as a prince hast thou power with God and with men, and hast prevailed" (Genesis 32:28). It applied to the family, tribe, nation, and race of which he was the progenitor.

Following the reign of Solomon, the ten northern tribes split off from Judah and Benjamin and founded the kingdom of Israel. This kingdom was destroyed by the Assyrians in 722 b.c. and its people carried into captivity. Literal Israel of today is the religious and social group called the Jewish people. "Behold, I will make them of the synagogue of Satan, which say they are Jews, and are not, but do lie; behold, I will make them to come and worship before thy feet, and to know that I have loved thee" (Revelation 3:9). Israel was the instrument of God to bring the light of the gospel of Christ to the world of His making.

Ephesians 2:11–22 — "Wherefore remember, that ye being in time past Gentiles in the flesh, who are called Uncircumcision by that which is called Circumcision in the flesh made by hands; That at that time ye were without Christ, being aliens from the commonwealth of Israel, and strangers from the covenants of promise, having no hope, and without God in the world: But now in Christ Jesus ye who sometimes were far off are made right by the blood of Christ. For he is our peace, who hath made both one, and hath broken down the middle wall of partition between us; Having abolished in his flesh the enmity, even the law of commandments contained in ordinances: for to make in himself of twain one new man, so making peace: And that he might reconcile both unto God in one body by the cross, having slain the enmity thereby: And came and preached peace to you which were afar off, and to them that were nigh. For through him we both have access by one Spirit unto the Father. Now therefore ye are no more strangers and foreigners, but fellow citizens with the saints, and of the household of God: And are built upon the foundation of the apostles and prophets, Jesus Christ himself being the chief cornerstone: In whom all the building fitly framed together groweth unto a holy temple in the Lord: In whom ye also are builded together for a habitation of God through the Spirit."

Isaiah 45:17, 25 — "But Israel shall be saved in the Lord with an everlasting salvation; ye shall not be ashamed nor confounded world without end. In the Lord shall all the seed of Israel be justified, and shall glory."

Isaiah 56:7, 8 — "Even them will I bring to my holy mountain, and make them joyful in my house of prayer; their burnt offerings and their sacrifices shall be accepted upon mine altar; for mine house shall be called a house of prayer for all people."

Galatians 3:24 — "The law was our schoolmaster to bring us unto Christ."

Galatians 6:15, 16 — "For in Christ Jesus neither circumcision availeth any thing, nor uncircumcision, but a new creature. And as many as walk according to this rule, peace be on them, and mercy, and upon the Israel of God."

Under the old covenant Israel was the wife of Jehovah. Isaiah 54:5 — "For thy maker is thine husband; the Lord of hosts is his name." She committed adultery. Ezekiel 16:31-32 — "In that thou buildest thine eminent place in the head of every way, and makest thine high place in every street; and hast not been as a harlot, in that thou scornest hire; but as a wife that committeth adultery, which taketh strangers instead of her husband!" See also the first two chapters of Hosea.

Now the church is wedded to Christ. John 3:29 — "He that hath the bride is the bridegroom: but the friend of the bridegroom, which standeth and heareth him, rejoiceth greatly because of the bridegroom's voice; this my joy therefore is fulfilled."

Ephesians 5:23–25 — "For the husband is the head of the wife, even as Christ is the head of the church: and he is the saviour of the body. Therefore as the church is subject unto Christ, so let the wives be to their husbands in every thing. Husbands, love your wives, even as Christ also loved the church, and gave himself for it."

Romans 7:2–3 — "For the woman which hath a husband is bound by the law to her husband so long as he liveth; but if the husband be dead, she is loosed from the law of her husband. So then if, while her husband liveth, she be married to another man, she shall be called an adulteress; but if her husband be dead, she is free from that law; so that she is no adulteress, though she be married to another man."

There will never be a restoration of the Jewish temple and sacrifices of animals for sin. Acts 4:12 — "Neither is there salvation in any other; for there is none other name under heaven given among men whereby we must be saved."

Hebrews 10:12 — "But this man, after he had offered *one sacrifice for sins forever,* sat down on the right hand of God."

John 10:9 — "I am the door; by me if any man enter in, he shall be saved." This opens the door wide for the literal Jew of today.

THE TRUE ISRAEL OF GOD

Chapter 2

THERE IS A LITERAL JEW AND A SPIRITUAL JEW

L et us look to Romans 2:28–29 — "For he is not a Jew, which is one outwardly; neither is that circumcision, which is outward in the flesh: But he is a Jew, which is one inwardly; and circumcision is that of the heart, in the spirit, and not in the letter; whose praise is not of men, but of God." No plainer definition could be given of who is the Israel of God today and hence his chosen people.

Romans 4:12–13 — And the father of circumcision to them who are not of the circumcision only, but who also walk in the steps of that faith of our father Abraham, which he had being yet uncircumcised. For the promise, that he should be the heir of the world, was not to Abraham, or to his seed, through the law, but through the righteousness of faith."

Romans 9:6 — "Not as though the word of God hath taken none effect. For they are not all Israel, which are of Israel."

Revelation 2:9 — "I know thy works, and tribulation, and poverty, but thou art rich and I know the blasphemy of them which say they are Jews, and are not, but are the synagogue of Satan" (See also Romans 11:1-32).

Galatians 3:7 — "Know ye therefore that they which are *of faith,* the same are the children of Abraham." (Or the Israel of God today.)

Galatians 3:26–29 — "For ye are all the children of God by faith in Christ Jesus. For as many of you as have been baptized into Christ have put on Christ. There is neither *Jew* nor *Greek,* there is neither bond nor free, there is neither male nor female; for ye are all one in Christ Jesus. And if ye be Christ's, then are ye Abraham's seed, and heir according to the promise."

Philippians 3:3 — "For we are the circumcision which worship God *in the spirit, and rejoice in Christ Jesus,* and have no confidence in the flesh."

The church is dear to God because He has *believing* and *obedient* saints. And only while this is so do they remain the chosen people of God. Are the Jews, who deny Christ, a holy nation today and the chosen people? No!

The spiritual nature of Israel began to emerge in the Old Testament. **Micah 6:6–8** — "Wherewith shall I come before the Lord, and bow myself before the high God? Shall I come before him with burnt offerings, with calves of a year old? Will the Lord be pleased with thousands of rams, or with ten thousands of rivers of oil? Shall I give my firstborn for my transgression, the fruit of my body for the sin of my soul? . . . What doth the Lord require of thee, but to do justly, and to love mercy, and to walk humbly with thy God."

Chapter 3

THE BIBLE NEVER LEAVES US IN THE DARK

Jesus forewarned of the transfer of citizenship from literal Israel to spiritual Israel. Matthew 21:43 — "Therefore I say unto you the kingdom of God shall be taken from you and given to a nation bringing forth the fruits thereof."

Mark 1:14-15 — "Now after that John was put in prison, Jesus came into Galilee, preaching the gospel of the kingdom of God, and saying, The time is fulfilled, and the kingdom of God is at hand; repent ye, and believe the gospel."

I Peter 2:9 — "But ye are a chosen generation, a royal priesthood, and holy nation, a peculiar people; that ye should shew forth the praises of him who hath called you out of darkness into his marvelous light; which in time past were not a people, but are now the people of God." You were not spiritual Israel, but you are now if you're born again.

Jesus denied the unbelieving Jews any place in the true

41

family of Abraham. John 8:39, 44 — "They answered and said unto him, Abraham is our father. Jesus saith unto them, If ye were Abraham's children, ye would do the works of Abraham. . . . Ye are of your father the devil, and the lusts of your father ye will do." "Now, if God has such special care for earthly (literal) Israel and if they are going to rule the world, would it not pay these various races—or any of us—to forsake Christ (for one must forsake him to become a Jew) and enter Judaism today while he can?" (C.E. Brown).

The Christian already has come to Zion (Jerusalem). Hebrews 12:22–23 — "But ye are come unto mount Zion, and unto the city of the living God, the heavenly Jerusalem, and to an innumerable company of angels, to the general assembly and church of the firstborn, which are written in heaven, and to God the Judge of all, and to the spirits of just men made perfect, and to Jesus the mediator of the new covenant, and to the blood of sprinkling, that speaketh better things than that of Abel." This is the Zion to which the true Israel was to be gathered "when the Lord shall bring again Zion" (Isaiah 52:8).

Ephesians 2:11–13, 19 — "Wherefore remember, that ye being in time past Gentiles in the flesh, who are called the uncircumcision by that which is called the circumcision in the flesh made by hands: That at that time ye were without Christ, being aliens from the commonwealth of Israel, and strangers from the covenants of promise, having no hope and without God in the world: But now in Christ Jesus ye who sometimes were far off are made nigh by the blood of Christ. . . . Now therefore ye are no more strangers and foreigners, but fellow-citizens with the saints, and of the household of God."

Christian believers certainly are members of Israel. Since they are not members of Judaism, Judaism today must not be Israel. If there be two Israels, then Christians belong to the *true Israel of God.*

First Peter 2:5 — "Ye also, as lively stones, are built up a *spiritual house.* an holy priesthood, to offer up spiritual sacrifices, acceptable to God by Jesus Christ." The Jews rejected Christ because he did not *literally* fulfill the prophecies as they had anticipated.

In Romans 10:1, Paul yearns for the salvation of Israel — "Brethren, my heart's desire and prayer to God for Israel is, that *they might be* saved." From this we cannot conclude that all of literal Israel will be saved. But we do read in Romans 10:9–13 how literal Israel can be saved: "That is thou shalt confess with thy mouth the Lord Jesus, and shall believe in thine heart that God hath raised him from the dead, thou shalt be saved." In Chapter 11 verse 5, Paul speaks of a remnant according to the election of *grace*. In verse 14 he speaks of saving *some* of them. In verse 20 he says, "Because of unbelief they were broken off." Verse 23 says, "And they also, if they abide not still in unbelief shall be grafted in."

In verse 25 Paul states, "For I would not, brethren, that ye should be ignorant of this mystery, lest ye should be wise in your own conceits: that blindness in part is happened to Israel, until the *fulness of the Gentiles* be come in." "This refers to the historical moment when Gentile Christians gained unequivocally their full freedom in the Christian church by complete victory over Jewish objections and no Jewish prejudice effectively hindered admission of Gentiles to the Israel of God" (Charles Ewing Brown).

Luke 21:24 — "And Jerusalem shall be trodden down of the Gentiles, until the times of the Gentiles be fulfilled." This happened in 70 a.d.

43

Chapter 4

THE KINGDOM OF GOD

Matthew 3:1-11 — "In those days came John the Baptist, preaching in the wilderness of Judea, and saying, Repent ye; for the kingdom of heaven is at hand. For this is he that was spoken of by the prophet Isaiah, saying, The voice of one crying in the wilderness, prepare ye the way of the Lord, make his paths straight. And the same John had his raiment of camel's hair, and a leathern girdle about his loins: and his meat was locust and wild honey. Then went out to him Jerusalem, and all Judea, and all the region round about Jordan, and were baptized of him in Jordan, confessing their sins. But when he saw many of the Pharisees and Sadducees come to his baptism, he said unto them, O generation of vipers, who hath warned you to flee from the wrath to come? Bring forth therefore fruits meet for repentance: And think not to say within yourselves, We have Abraham to our father; for I say unto you, that God is able of these stones to raise up children unto

Abraham. And now also the axe is laid unto the root of the trees: therefore every tree which bringeth not forth good fruit is hewn down, and cast into the fire. I indeed baptize you with water unto repentance; but he that cometh after me is mightier than I, whose shoes I am not worthy to bear: he shall baptize you with the Holy Ghost, and with fire."

Romans 14:17 — "For the kingdom of God is not meat and drink; but righteousness, and peace, and joy in the Holy Ghost."

Mark 9:1 — "And he said unto them, Verily I say unto you, That there be some of them that stand here, which shall not taste of death, till they have seen the kingdom of God come with power."

The kingdom of God differs radically from all kingdoms of this world by not having a human king sitting on a great throne-seat. Instead, Jesus sits on his throne in the life of each individual person who has been saved and sanctified (born again and filled with the Holy Spirit).

True, the Hebrews were the chosen people to reveal Jehovah and bring forth the Messiah, but God does not rule over a particular nationality, but over those who have been born from above and are in Paul's words, "of the Spirit."

I want to speak of this kingdom. Jesus' teaching in Luke 17:20, 21 says, "And when he was demanded of the Pharisees, when the kingdom of God should come, he answered them and said, The kingdom of God cometh not with observation: Neither shall they say, Lo here! or, lo there! for, behold, the kingdom of God is within you." (Note also Moffatt's *Reign of God*.)

Romans 14:1, 2 — "Him that is weak in the faith receive ye, but not to doubtful disputations. For one believeth that he may eat all things; another, who is weak, eateth herbs." See the difference between the essential and the nonessential in Christianity.

The essence of God's reign does not consist in feasting or fasting. Many there are who sincerely believe that the eating of certain foods on certain days or the abstaining from the eating of certain foods is an evidence of righteousness in the heart.

Mark 7:18-23 — "And he saith unto them, Are ye so without understanding also? Do ye not perceive, that whatsoever thing from without entereth into the man, it cannot defile him; because it entereth not into his heart, but into the belly, and goeth out into the draught, purging all meats? And he said, That which cometh out of the man, that defileth the man. For from within, out of the heart of men, proceed evil thoughts, adulteries, fornications, murders, thefts, covetousness, wickedness, deceit, lasciviousness, and evil eye, blasphemy, pride, foolishness: All these evil things come from within, and defile the man."

I was once with a minister who told me, "During Lent I have given up meat, bread, and coffee." During the hour he drank four beers and smoked a pack of cigarettes. No doubt many of us would benefit if we gave up bread and other food. Certainly medical research and the cancer society have established that nicotine causes cancer and heart trouble, and excessive use of alcohol is one of the prime problems of the day. However, abstaining from all these is not the Kingdom of God.

A man aboard a ship was called to dinner. Jews could not eat it because it was pork, and Catholics could not because it was a Friday. Mohammedans could not eat the sauce The only person present who could eat the meal was a converted Indian. Did Jesus die that our menus be changed?

The essence of the Kingdom of God consists in neither costumes or customs. World travelers photograph the world's religious costumes and differences: golden-robed Buddhists at the Temple of Dawn and the Hindu priests of Calcutta; pilgrims at St. Peter's Square in Rome and Amish schoolchildren in Iowa; the long-haired Israelites of Benton Harbor and the mountain holiness groups in black dress. Was the incarnation designed to bring about a change in garment? The Kingdom of God consists of neither statues or steeples, holidays or holy days. Is the missionary task of the church to change architecture or calendars? Would the Near East suddenly become Christian if all the mosques were replaced with gothic cathedrals? Was heaven pleased that our bombers avoided the Holy City to save its art but released the bombs on men?

What is the temple of God? I Corinthians 3:16 — "Know ye not that ye are the temple of God, and that the Spirit of God dwelleth in you?"

I Corinthians 6:19 — "What? Know ye not that your body is the temple of the Holy Ghost which is in you, which ye have of God, and ye are not your own?" The Kingdom of God is not a limited territorial sovereignty, nor is it geographically defined. It is not ushered in with great parades and flying banners.

Romans 14:17 — "For the kingdom of God is not meat and drink; but righteousness, and peace, and joy in the Holy Ghost." The essence of the reign of God on earth consists of a spiritual experience with Jesus Christ wrought by the Holy Spirit.

Romans 5:1 — "Therefore being justified by faith, we have peace with God through our Lord Jesus Christ." This is the central text in all of Paul's teachings. All great preaching is rooted in the doctrine of justification by faith.

Romans 8:1: "There is therefore now no condemnation to them which are in Christ Jesus, who walk not after the flesh, but after the Spirit."

A couple visited a minister in the west. "My impression of the man had been that he was a playboy, of the ultrasophisticated variety. He was brilliant but had no real earnestness. His wife seemed under a strain. After greeting they immediately requested to see the minister alone. In a serious, troubled way, the man said, 'We have come here in the hope that you will guide us into a more satisfying way of life. Mary is half sick almost all the time, we never seem to get her well. As for me, I'm in good shape physically, but just as miserable. I just don't feel I am making my life count for anything. I'm not happy at all. We can't go on this way. We thought you might be able to help us.'" Said the minister, "I doubt that I can help you. You may be too sophisticated and complicated for my simple way. But I can tell you where you can get help." The husband replied, "You want to refer us to someone else?" To which the minister replied, "I want to refer you to the Bible, but I wonder if you have what it takes to try it." They both looked startled and the man asked, "Why do you say that?" "Because your approach to life seems to be very superficial," replied the minister.

The following spring a letter came for the minister. It was joyous, almost a lyrical burst of self-expression. "Never have I had such a springtime. Never has the grass seemed greener, the flowers more beautiful, the sky bluer, sunshine more golden, or life more alive. Mary's health is so much better that she is a different person. God has come into our lives. We both have been saved and sanctified."

In 1897 Barney E. Warren wrote a song titled "The Kingdom of Peace." "There's a theme that is sweet to my mem'ry; there's a joy that I cannot express; there's a treasure that gladdens my being; 'Tis the Kingdom of God's righteousness. 'Tis a Kingdom of peace, it is reigning within, it shall ever increase in my soul; We possess it right here when He saves us from all sin, and 'twill last while the ages shall roll."

Isaiah 9:6-7 — "For unto us a child is born, unto us a son is given; and the government shall be upon his shoulder: and his name shall be called Wonderful, Counselor, the mighty God, the everlasting Father, the Prince of Peace. Of the increase of his government and peace there shall be no end, upon the throne of David, and upon his kingdom, to order it, and to establish it with judgment and with justice from hence forth even for ever. The zeal of the Lord of hosts will perform this." This does not come by climbing holy stairs. . . .

Titus 2:11, 12 — "For the grace of God that bringeth salvation hath appeared to all men. Teaching us that, denying ungodliness and worldly lusts, we should live soberly, righteously, and godly, in this present world."

Titus 3:5–6 — "Which he shed on us abundantly through Jesus Christ our Savior; that being justified by his grace, we should be made heirs according to the hope of eternal life." In the words of Saint Augustine, "Had I all the faith of the patriarchs, all the zeal of the martyrs, and the flaming devotion of seraphs, I would disclaim them all in point of dependence, and rely only on free grace. I would count all but dross when put in competition with the infinitely precious death and meritorious righteousness of my dear Savior Jesus Christ; and, if ever a true reformation of life is produced, it must be produced by *free grace*. Till this doctrine is generally inculcated, the most excellent harangues from the pulpit, or the most correct dissertations from the press, will be no better than a pointless arrow or a broken bow."

We say the Kingdom is a spiritual kingdom in that it is governed through the agency of the Holy Spirit. It was ushered in with power on the day of Pentecost with the coming of the Holy Spirit into the hearts of believers, cleansing them of sin and placing Christ upon His throne. Jesus came preaching and healing in the power of the Spirit. "Behold the Kingdom of God is within you." He promised the church through the disciples that He would send the Holy Spirit into our hearts to serve as our personal Comforter, Companion, Counselor, Co-witness, Convictor, and Conductor. It is the Holy Spirit that sets the members in the Kingdom in the way it pleases Him.

I Corinthians 12:18 — "But now hath God set the members every one of them in the body, as it hath pleased him." Without Him, we may be in the church, but not in the Kingdom. So the Kingdom of God is that realm in which the Holy Spirit dominates.

There are two cleansings. The first takes away all sins committed. Revelation 1:5 — "And from Jesus Christ, who is the faithful witness, and the first begotten of the dead, and the prince of the kings of the earth. Unto him that loved us, and washed us from our sins in his own blood." The second purifies our hearts from inborn sin. 1 John 1:8, 9 — "If we say that we have no sin, we deceive ourselves, and the truth is not in us. If we confess our sins, he is faithful and just to forgive us our sins, and to cleanse us from all unrighteousness." The two cleansings are termed justification and sanctification.

Luke 18:13, 14 — "And the publican, standing afar off, would not lift up so much as his eyes unto heaven, but smote upon his breast, saying, God be merciful to me a sinner. I tell you, this man went down to his house justified rather than the other: for every one that exalteth himself shall be abased; and he that humbleth himself shall be exalted."

Romans 4:5 — "But to him that worketh not, but believeth on him that justifieth the ungodly, his faith is counted for righteousness."

I Thessalonians 4:3 — "For this is the will of God, even your sanctification, that ye should abstain from fornication." The first is to the sinner, the second to the believer.

John 17:17–20 — "Sanctify them through thy truth; thy word is truth. As thou hast sent me into the world, even so have I also sent them into the world. And for their sakes I sanctify myself, that they also might be sanctified through the truth. Neither pray I for these alone, but for them also which shall believe on me through their word."

First Thessalonians 1:1; 4:1–3: "Paul, and Silvanus, and Timothy, unto the church of the Thessalonians which is in God the Father and in the Lord Jesus Christ: Grace be unto you, and peace, from God our Father, and the Lord Jesus Christ. Furthermore then we beseech you, brethren, and exhort you by the Lord Jesus, that as ye have received of us how ye ought to walk and to please God, so ye would abound more and more. For ye know what commandments we gave you by the Lord Jesus.

For this is the will of God, even your sanctification, that ye should abstain from fornication."

John 15:2 — "Every branch in me that beareth not fruit he taketh away: and every branch that beareth fruit, he purgeth it, that it may bring forth more fruit." This is conferred not by subscribing to an eclectical dogma. It is conferred by Jesus Christ, when we are willing to let Him be King, and us His subjects.

The Kingdom of God consists in peace. Galatians 5:22–23 — "But the fruit of the Spirit is love, joy, peace, long-suffering, gentleness, goodness, faith, meekness, temperance: against such there is no law."

The Kingdom of God consists of joy. When the Kingdom of God came at Pentecost, the disciples were so happy and rejoiced so much the people said, "These folks are drunk on new wine." Peter said, "This is that." How quickly and spontaneously the early Christians broke out in song! From the sewers and catacombs of Rome they rejoiced because of the lively hope of eternal life. Inspired by God, in 1900 Barney E. Warren wrote the hymn, "There Is Joy in the Lord." "I will sing hallelujah for there's joy in the Lord, and He fills my heart with rapture as I rest on His Word; I will trust in His promise. I will shout I am free, in my blessed loving Savior I have sweet victory. There is joy in the Lord, there is joy in the Lord; Hallelujah, glory, glory! There is joy in the Lord. There is joy in the Lord, there is joy in the Lord; Hallelujah, glory, glory! There is joy in the Lord."

Conclusion

The great fundamental teaching of the Kingdom of God is this: Man can come to know the truth and thereby change! You don't have to remain as you are! Again and again I have seen people with all kinds of frustrations, defeats, conflicts, mixed-up, miserable, unhappy, and defeated. I have seen them recognize their failures and come to Jesus Christ and seek the Holy Spirit until He comes in, and He had *changed them.*

God is a God of righteousness. Man gets full of sin, but Jesus died for His redemption. The Holy Spirit abides to live with him. This is the essence of the Kingdom of God.

Christianity can be called the everlasting springtime of the soul, with growth and potential and infinite development, looking toward the coming of the harvest both here and beyond.

It is a great faith. Take it to your heart. Live by it. Give yourself to it. It's the greatest thing in life.

Chapter 5

THY KINGDOM COME

John 18:6 — "My kingdom is not of this world: If my kingdom were of this would my servants fight." The Jews expected that when their Messiah came he would establish a literal earthly kingdom. They placed a literal interpretation upon the prophecies concerning Him. They expected Him to have a temporal throne, to subdue the nations, and to restore again the Kingdom of Israel with all the glory it had under David. This gross error led them to reject Christ, oppose His spiritual Kingdom, and to consent to His death.

At one time they tried by force to take Him and make Him a king. John 6:14-15 — "Then those men, when they had seen the miracle that Jesus did, said, This is of a truth that prophet that should come into the world. When Jesus therefore perceived that they would come and take him by force, to make him a king, he departed again unto a mountain himself alone." Wanting only an earthly king, they rejected and crucified Christ.

Prophecies Concerning the Kingdom

Daniel 2:44 — "And in the days of these kings shall the God of heaven set up a kingdom which shall never be destroyed; and the kingdom shall not be left to other people, but it shall break in pieces and consume all these kingdoms, and it shall stand for ever." (The last of these four kingdoms of Daniel 2 was the Roman Empire, during which Christ came.) The image the king saw in his dream was the complete figure of a man, every part of which was in proportion to the whole image.

Isaiah 9:6–7 — "For unto us a child is born, unto us a son is given, and the government shall be upon his shoulder; and His name shall be called Wonderful, Counsellor, the Mighty God, the Everlasting Father, the Prince of Peace. Of the increase of His government and peace there shall be no end, upon the throne of David, and upon his kingdom, to order it, and to establish it with judgment and with justice, from henceforth even forever."

Luke 1:30-33 — The angel Gabriel said to Mary, ". . . and shalt call his name Jesus. He shall be great, and shall be called the Son of the Highest: and the Lord God shall give unto him the throne of his father David; and shall reign over the house of Jacob forever; and of his kingdom there shall be no end" That which was spoken by Daniel was fulfilled in Christ's first coming.

Mark 1:14-15 — "Now after that John was put in prison, Jesus came into Galilee preaching the gospel of the kingdom of God, and saying, the time is fulfilled [spoken by Daniel], and the kingdom of God is at hand. Repent ye, and believe the gospel." The terms *kingdom of God* and *kingdom of heaven* are used interchangeably.

Matthew 4:17 — "From that time Jesus began to preach, and to say, Repent; for the kingdom of heaven is at hand."

Mark 1:15 — "And saying, The time is fulfilled, and the kingdom of God is at hand; repent ye, and believe the gospel."

Matthew 13:24 — "Another parable put he forth unto them, saying, The kingdom of heaven is likened unto a man which sowed good seed in his field."

Mark 4:30 — "And he said, Whereunto shall we liken the kingdom of God? or with what comparison shall we compare it?"

Matthew 11:11 — "Verily I say unto you, Among them that are born of women there hath not risen a greater than John the Baptist; notwithstanding he that is least in the kingdom of heaven is greater than he."

Luke 7:28 — "For I say unto you, Among those that are born of women there is not a greater prophet than John the Baptist; but he that is least in the kingdom of God is greater than he." "At hand" refers not something that is hundreds of years away, but something that is close to or available now.

Matthew 3:1-2 — "In those days came John the Baptist preaching in the wilderness of Judea, and saying, Repent ye; for the kingdom of heaven is at hand."

Matthew 4:17 — "From that time Jesus began to preach, and to say, Repent; for the kingdom of heaven is at hand."

Matthew 4:23 — "And Jesus went about all Galilee, teaching in their synagogues, and preaching the gospel of the kingdom, and healing all manner of sickness and all manner of disease among the people." Why preach it? It was "at hand."

Nature of the Kingdom

Matthew 5:3 — "Blessed are the poor in Spirit, for theirs is the kingdom of heaven."

Matthew 8:12 — "Except ye be converted and become as little children, ye shall not enter into the kingdom of heaven." Jesus said to Nicodemus in John 3:3, "Verily, verily, I say unto thee, except a man be born again, he cannot see the kingdom of God."

Matthew 6:33 — "But seek ye first the kingdom of God, and his righteousness, and all these things [food, drink, clothing] shall be added unto you." They were to seek for it then. It was obtainable then.

Pilate asked Jesus if he was king of the Jews. Jesus answered, "My kingdom is not of this world; if my kingdom were of this world, then would my servants fight." Luke 17:20–21 — "And when he was demanded of the Pharisees, when the kingdom of God should come, he answered them and said, The kingdom of God cometh not with observation: Neither shall they say, Lo here! [Jerusalem] or, lo there! for, behold, the kingdom of God is within you." When you are "born again" into the family, He becomes your King.

Luke 18:18–26 — "And a certain ruler asked him, saying, Good Master, what shall I do to inherit eternal life? And Jesus said unto him, Why callest thou me good? none is good, save one, that is, God. Thou knowest the commandments, Do not commit adultery, Do not kill, Do not steal, Do not bear false witness, Honor thy father and thy mother. And he said, All these have I kept from my youth up. Now when Jesus heard these things, he said unto him, Yet lackest thou one thing: sell all that thou hast, and distribute unto the poor, and thou shalt have treasure in heaven: and come, follow me. And when he heard this, he was very sorrowful: for he was very rich. And when Jesus saw that he was very sorrowful, he said, How hardly shall they that have riches enter into the kingdom of God! For it is easier for a camel to go through a needle's eye, than for a rich man to enter into the kingdom of God. And they that heard it said, Who then can be saved?" Here we see the kingdom and salvation classed together in the minds of the people.

Matthew 23:13 — "But woe unto you, scribes and Pharisees, hypocrites! for ye shut up the kingdom of heaven against men; for ye neither go in yourselves, neither suffer ye them that are entering to go in."

Now we look at Paul's definition of the kingdom. Romans 14:17 — "For the kingdom of God is not meat and drink [earthly]; but righteousness, and peace, and joy in the Holy Ghost [spiritual]."

This peace, righteousness and joy come by faith. Romans 5:1 — "Therefore being justified by faith we have peace with God through our Lord Jesus Christ."

The Kingdom is not in a future age or time. It has already been set up and people are now reigning with Christ in it.

Jesus said to the multitude, "Fear not, little flock; for it is your Father's good pleasure to give you the kingdom" (Luke 12:32). When? Some future age? No! Right then!

Matthew 11:12 — "And from the days of John the Baptist until now the kingdom of heaven suffereth violence, and the violent take it by force." Then in Matthew 12 Jesus was accused of casting out devils by the Prince of devils. He answers this accusation in verse 28: "But if I cast out devils by the Spirit of God, then the kingdom of God is come unto you." Did He?? Did it??

And again in Mark 9:1 He said unto them, "Verily I say unto you, That there be some of them that stand here, which shall not taste of death, till they have seen the kingdom of God come with power." When with power? "Ye shall receive power after that the Holy Ghost is come upon you" (Acts 1:8).

Luke 16:16-17 — "The law and the prophets were until John; since that time the kingdom of God is preached, and every man presseth into it. And it is easier for heaven and earth to pass, than one tittle of the law to fail."

The disciples were commissioned to preach the kingdom of God and heal the sick. Luke 9:2 — "And he sent them to preach the kingdom of God, and to heal the sick." One was as real then as the other.

They were in the Kingdom then. "Who [Father] hath delivered us from the power of darkness [sin], and hath translated [changed from one condition to another] us into the kingdom of his dear Son" (Colossians 1:13).

Revelation 1:9 — "I, John, who also am your brother, and companion in tribulation, and in the kingdom and patience of Jesus Christ, was in the isle that is called Patmos, for the word of God, and for the testimony of Jesus Christ."

The reign of God's saints on earth is a present reality. It is the spiritual rule of God in the hearts of his people. It is a "within" kingdom. It is spiritual in nature. We enter it through spiritual means.

Revelation 1:5b, 6 — "Unto him that loved us, and washed us from our sins in his own blood. And hath made us kings and priests unto God and his Father; to him be glory and dominion for ever and ever. Amen."

Revelation 5:10 — "And hast made us unto our God kings and priests; and we shall reign on the earth."

Romans 5:17 — "For if by one man's offense death reigned by one; much more they which receive abundance of grace and of the gift of righteousness shall reign in life by one, Jesus Christ."

Romans 6:14 — "For sin shall not have dominion over you; for ye are not under the law, but under grace."

I John 5:4 — "Whosoever is born of God, *overcometh the world*." That is reigning. Luke 10:19 — "Behold I give unto you power to tread on serpents and scorpions, and *over all the power* of the enemy; and nothing shall by any means hurt you." That is reigning and Satan is not bound while you are reigning over him.

There Will Be No Time or Place for Another Kingdom When Christ Returns

Hebrews 1:1-2 — "In these *last days* he hath spoken unto us by his Son."

I John 2:18-19 — "Little children, it is *the last time*."

Matthew 24:14 — "And this *gospel of the kingdom* shall be preached in all the world for a witness unto all nations; and then shall *the end* come."

II Thessalonians 1:7-10 — ". . . when the Lord Jesus shall be revealed from heaven with his mighty angels . . . taking vengeance on them that know not God, and that obey not the gospel of our Lord Jesus Christ . . . when he shall come to be glorified in his saints."

I Corinthians 15:24 — "Then cometh the end, when he shall have *delivered up the kingdom* to God."

I John 2:18 — "Little children, *it is the last time*; and as ye have heard that antichrist shall come, *even now* are there many antichrists; Note that it is not *the* Antichrist) whereby we know that *it is the last time*."

I Thessalonians 4:16 — "For *the Lord Himself shall descend from heaven* with a shout, with the voice of the archangel, and with *the trump of God;* and the dead in Christ shall rise first; then we which are alive and remain shall be caught together with them in the clouds."

I Corinthians 15:50–52; "Now this I say, brethren, that *flesh and blood* cannot inherit *the kingdom of God* [future]; neither doth corruption inherit incorruption. Behold, I shew you a mystery; we shall not all sleep, but we shall all be changed, in a moment, in the twinkling of an eye, *at the last trump,* (which sounds at Christ's next coming) for the trump shall sound, and *the dead shall be raised* incorruptible, and we shall be changed." There is no trump after *the last trump*.

Revelation 10:5-7 — ". . . there should be *time no longer;* but in the days of the voice of the seventh angel, when he shall begin to sound [trump] the mystery of God should be *finished,* as he hath declared to his servants and prophets."

Revelation 11:15 — "And the seventh angel sounded, and there were great voices in heaven saying, The *kingdoms of this world* are *become the kingdoms of our Lord,* and of his Christ; and he shall reign for ever and ever."

At this time, when Christ comes, when the last trump sounds, this world passes away forever. II Peter 3:3–14 — "Knowing this first, that there shall come in the last days scoffers, walking after their own lusts, and saying, Where is the promise of his coming? for since the fathers fell asleep, all things continue as they were from the beginning of the creation. For this they willingly are ignorant of, that by the word of God the heavens were of old, and the earth standing out of the water and in the water: Whereby the world that then was, being overflowed with water, perished; But the heavens and the earth, which are now, by the same word are kept in store, reserved unto fire against the day of judgment and perdition of ungodly men. But, beloved, be not ignorant of this one thing, that one day is with the Lord as a thousand years, and a thousand years at one day. The Lord is not slack concerning his promise, as some men count slackness; but is long-suffering to us-ward, not willing that any should perish, but that all should come to repentance. But *the day of the Lord* [Christ's second coming] will come as a thief in the night; in the which *the heavens shall pass away* with a great noise, and *the elements shall melt with fervent heat, the earth also* and the works that are therein *shall be burned up.* Seeing then that all these things shall be dissolved, what manner of persons ought ye to be in all holy conversation and godliness. Looking for and hasting unto the coming of the day of God, wherein the heavens being on fire shall be dissolved, and the elements shall melt with fervent heat? Nevertheless we, according to his promise, look for new heavens and a new earth, wherein dwelleth righteousness. Wherefore, beloved, seeing that ye look for such things, be diligent that ye may be found of him in peace, without spot, and blameless."

Yes, there will be *no time nor place* for a future earthly kingdom when Jesus comes again.

II Peter 1:10-11 — "Wherefore the rather, brethren, give diligence to make your calling and election sure: for if ye do these things, ye shall never fall; for so an entrance shall be ministered unto you abundantly into *the everlasting kingdom* of our Lord and Saviour Jesus Christ."

Heaven begins for the believer when he by faith and repentance enters God's Kingdom. If we expect to reign with Him hereafter, then He must here and now reign in us. (Quote from Max R. Gaulke).

THE TRUE ISRAEL OF GOD

Chapter 6

THE ANTICHRIST AND MAN OF SIN

The millennial theory teaches that Antichrist is to be manifested during the great tribulation that follows Christ's rapture with the saints.

What does the Scripture say? Second Thessalonians 2:2-8 — "That ye be not soon shaken in mind, or be troubled, neither by spirit, nor by word, nor by letter as from us, as that the day of Christ is at hand. Let no man deceive you by any means; for that day shall not come, except there come a falling away first, and that man of sin be revealed, the son of perdition who opposeth and exalteth himself above all that is called God, showing himself that he is God. Remember ye not, that, when I was yet with you, I told you these things? And now ye know what withholdeth that he might be revealed in his time. For the mystery of iniquity doth already work: only he who now letteth will let, until he be taken out of the way. And then shall that wicked be revealed whom the Lord shall consume with the spirit of his mouth, and shall destroy with the brightness of his coming." That Paul was not telling of some half-man and half-devil who was to arise more than two thousand years later and contend with people left on earth after Christ's people had been taken up is perfectly apparent. The apostasy and the man of sin were to be *a sign to the Christians* before they should expect Christ to return. If Christ were to snatch them away before the appearance of the man of sin so they would not be on earth at this manifestation, how could the revealing of the man of sin be any sign to them of the approach of the coming of the Lord? But Paul tells the Christians not to expect the day of Christ until *after* the manifestation of the man of sin. Paul said the "mystery of iniquity" was at work in his lifetime.

That the papacy was the manifestation of the man of sin was held by Savonarola, the Albigenses, the Waldenses, Wycliffe, the Hussites, Saint Bernard, Martin Luther, Calvin, Zwingli, and others too numerous to mention. It is an article in the creed of the Lutheran church that the pope is Antichrist. The same doctrine is also part of the Westminster Confession — the creed of Presbyterianism. In the dedication in the front of the King James Bible, the translators expressed their thanks to King James for writing against the "man of sin," by which they meant the papacy. However, we cannot today confine this just to the papacy.

I John 2:18 — "Little children, it is the last time: and as ye have heard that the antichrist shall come, *even now are there many antichrists*: whereby we know that it is the last time." He says there were many in his day, 2000 years ago, not just one. He tells us how to discern antichrist under whatever guise he may appear: "Every spirit that confesseth not that Jesus Christ is come in the flesh is not of God: and this is that spirit of antichrist, whereof ye have heard that it should come; and even *now already* is it in the world" (I John 4:3). And again he says in II John 7, "For many deceivers are entered into the world, who confess not that Jesus Christ is come in the flesh. This is a deceiver and an antichrist." For example, Christian Science, with its denial of the essential deity and true fleshly nature of Jesus Christ, is a picture of the antichrist in religion. And so is every religious teacher who denies that Jesus Christ is God in human flesh.

Chapter 7

THE GREAT TRIBULATION

Accoring to the premillennial theory, the Great Tribulation will come upon the earth during the seven-year period between the second and third comings of Christ while the saints are caught away from the earth with Christ. Certainly the church will pass through the tribulation that Christ speaks of. He said in John 16:33, "In the world ye shall have tribulation." Paul taught in Acts 14:22 that we "must through much tribulation enter into the kingdom of God."

Romans 12:12 — "Rejoicing in hope; patient in tribulation; continuing instant in prayer."

Second Corinthians 1:4 — "Who comforteth us in all our tribulation, that we may be able to comfort them which are in any trouble, by the comfort wherewith we ourselves are comforted of God."

I Thessalonians 3:4 — "For verily, when we were with you, we told you before that we should suffer tribulation; even as it came to pass, and ye know."

Revelation 1:9 — "I John, who also am your brother, and companion in tribulation." All the redeemed in heaven "are white in the blood of the Lamb" (Revelation 7:14).

The Bible nowhere speaks of *"the"* great tribulation. Christians of all ages have passed through great tribulations whether it be the siege of Jerusalem under Titus, the martyrdom of 5.5 million during the reign of the papacy, the persecution of the Communists in all Communist-controlled countries, or living a devoted Christian life in the United States today.

Chapter 8

ARMAGEDDON AND GOG AND MAGOG

Revelation 16:13-16 — "And I saw three unclean spirits like frogs come out of the mouth of the dragon, and out of the mouth of the beast, and out of the mouth of the false prophet. For they are the spirits of devils, working miracles, which goeth forth unto the kings of the earth and of the whole world, to gather them to the battle of that great day of God Almighty. Behold, I come as a thief. Blessed is he that watcheth, and keepeth his garments, lest he walk naked, and they see his shame. And he gathered them together into a place called in the Hebrew tongue Armageddon." This takes us back to the plain of Megiddo in Old Testament history. The plain was famous for two great slaughters, that of the Canaanitish host of Barak celebrated in the song of Deborah, and that in which King Josiah fell. Here, too, was the victory of Gideon over the Midianites. (See Judges 4, 5 and 7.)

From this passage many premillennialists actually see a

future literal batter between God and the hosts of antichrist. They say there will be 200,000,000 horsemen in their army. This will be on a tract of ground forty miles long and 20 miles wide. Think of this kind of army going to battle with this kind of equipment in this modern age. Besides that, it would be impossible to get 200,000,000 horses on that size piece of ground. The important thing to see is not the place but the demand God lays upon His people to be holy. "The most that can be reliably said concerning a battle of Armageddon is that the Bible facts indicate two powers present in the world up to the time of the second coming of Christ. First the elect will continue to be gathered into the Church, thus increasing steadily the total number of regenerated believers. Second, the forces of evil grow worse and worse in the world as Satan in his madness uses every power at his command to overthrow the church of God" (Max Gaulke). "Armageddon is not as some have supposed, a battle fought with lead and steel, but *a struggle between the powers of right and wrong*" (Lawrence Chesnut).

The true biblical church of God is a spiritual institution and is not an army that fights literal battles. Her members are saved from sin and hatred. Jesus said, "Love your enemies, bless them that curse you, do good to them that hate you and pray for them which despitefully use you, and persecute you" (Matthew 5:44). According to God's Word, Christians should not kill or avenge themselves. Jesus said in Luke 3:14, "Do violence to no man." Paul says in Ephesians 6:12, "We wrestle not against flesh and blood, but against principalities, against powers, against the rulers of the darkness of this world, against spiritual wickedness in high places."

Second Corinthians 10:4 — "*For the weapons of our warfare are not carnal*, but mighty through God to the pulling down of strongholds."

Ephesians 4:31–32 — "Let all bitterness, and wrath, and anger, and clamor, and evil speaking, be put away from you, with all malice: and be ye kind one to another, tenderhearted, forgiving one another, even as God for Christ's sake hath forgiven you."

Ephesians 5:1–2 — "Be ye therefore followers of God, as dear children: And walk in love, as Christ also hath loved us, and hath given himself for us an offering and a sacrifice to God for a sweet smelling savor."

Romans 12:21 — "Be not overcome of evil, but overcome evil with good."

Let's look to Revelation 19:11–16 to see the leader of his army: "And I saw heaven opened, and behold a white horse; and he that sat upon him was called Faithful and True, and in righteousness he doth judge and make war. His eyes were as a flame of fire, and on his head were many crowns; and he had a name written, that no man knew, but he himself. And he was clothed with a vesture dipped in blood: and his name is called The Word of God. And the armies which were in heaven followed him upon white horses, clothed in fine linen, white and clean. And out of his mouth goeth a sharp sword, that with it he should smite the nations: and he shall rule them with a rod of iron: and he treadeth the winepress of the fierceness and wrath of Almighty God. And he hath on his vesture and on his thigh a name written, King of kings, and Lord of lords." In verse 11 a white horse is spoken of, a symbol of an army, warrior and warfare. The rider is Christ. And *in righteousness* (not carnal, literal warfare) he doth judge and make war. His *warfare is on the plain of righteousness, not physical combat*. The armies in verse 14 are the saints of God that compose God's true church here on earth. They were also on white horses, meaning they too were in this righteous warfare with Christ as their captain. The fine linen is the righteousness of the saints. In verse 15 it shows the Word of Christ going forth from His mouth.

Hebrews 12:4 — "Ye have not yet resisted unto blood, striving against sin."

73

Ephesians 6:17 — "And take the helmet of salvation, and the sword of the Spirit, which is the word of God." The rod of iron. His Word. He treadeth the winepress. . . . He sends judgment on all that refuse to obey His Word, and all on that reject it.

Revelation 19:19 — "And I saw the beast, and the kings of the earth, and their armies gathered together to make war against him that sat on the horse, and against his army." Here God revealed to John that all false religions would gather themselves together near the end of time to make war against Christ and His Church. This also comes out in Revelation 20:7-8 — "And when the thousand years are expired, Satan shall be loosed out of his prison, and shall go out to deceive the nations which are in the four quarters of the earth, Gog and Magog, to gather them together to battle; the number of whom is as the sand of the sea." This is another word picture of the condition near the end of the world. The great trend of the world is against God, His Word, His church, and all forms of true Christianity.

Also interesting is the 38th and 39th chapters of Ezekiel. Much is made of these tribes of the Old Testament time being Russia coming down from the north against Israel. But note they are all riding horses and carrying all sorts of armor foreign to our day and times — bucklers, shields, swords, bows and arrows, handstaves, and spears (verses four and nine in chapter 39). Strange weapons and warfare for the Russia of today or of the future.

Adam Clarke ascribes this either to Cambyses, king of Persia, or Antiochus Epiphanes, king of Syria. Antiochus defiled the Jewish temple by offering a sow for a sacrifice on the altar (abomination of desolation of Daniel).

74

Chapter 9

THE RAPTURE

This word is not found in the Bible, yet the idea of it is taught in I Thessalonians 4:13–17 and in I Corinthians 15:51–53. What is meant by the world *rapture* is the sudden and possibly secret coming of Christ in the air to catch away from the earth the resurrected bodies of those who have died in the faith and with them the living saints, leaving the unrighteous dead and living behind. It is taught by many that suddenly and invisibly, without being seen by the unrighteous, the Lord will come as a thief in the night and steal away His waiting saints. They say that the unsaved will discover that their believing wives, daughters, or sons (what about the men?) have disappeared. When they start looking around they will find others looking for their loved ones who have disappeared. This would definitely call for a third coming of Christ. We will see in our next chapter what happens when Christ returns.

Chapter 10

THE KINGDOM DELIVERED UP (NOT SET UP) WHEN CHRIST RETURNS

First Corinthians 15:24 — "Then cometh the end, when he shall have delivered up the kingdom to God, even the Father." The coming of Christ will be the end of all hope for sinners.

II Thessalonians 1:7–9, "The Lord Jesus shall be revealed from heaven with his mighty angels, in flaming fire taking vengeance on them that know not God . . . who shall be punished with everlasting destruction from the presence of the Lord."

I Corinthians 11:26 — "For as often as ye eat this bread, and drink this cup, ye do show the Lord's death, *till he come.*" When the Lord comes the gospel ministry will come to an end. No more sinners converted, no more saints warned, no more ordinances administered. Beyond that is eternity with the Lord or without the Lord. The apostasy and the man of sin were to be a sign to the Christians before they should expect Christ. Now if Christ were to come and snatch away the Christians before the appearance of the man of sin, so that they would not even be on earth at his manifestation, how could the revelation of the man of sin be any sign to them of the approach of the coming of the Lord? The Bible plainly sets forth all that will happen when Jesus comes again. Let's look at the teaching on this subject that all can understand.

In Acts 1:11 the angels announced, "This same Jesus, which is taken up from you into heaven, shall so come *in like manner* as ye have seen him go into heaven."

Hebrews 9:28 — "Unto them that look for him shall he appear *the second time*." The Scripture teaches that there is but one personal coming of Christ in the future.

Matthew 24:3 — "What shall be the sign *of thy coming*?"

II Thessalonians 2:1 — "Now we beseech you, brethren, by *the coming* of our Lord Jesus Christ."

I Thessalonians 5:23 — "Preserved blameless unto *the coming* of our Lord Jesus Christ."

Titus 2:13 — "Looking for that blessed hope, and *the glorious appearing* of the great God and our Saviour Jesus Christ."

I John 2:28 — "And now, little children, abide in him: that, when he shall appear, we may have confidence, and not be ashamed before him at his coming."

James 5:7–8 — "Be patient therefore, brethren, unto the coming of the Lord. Behold, the husbandman waiteth for the precious fruit of the earth, and hath long patience for it, until he receive the early and latter rain. Be ye also patient: stablish your hearts; for the coming of the Lord draweth nigh."

His Coming Is Going to Be Visible to All, Both Saved and Unsaved

Revelation 1:7 — "Behold, he cometh with clouds: and *every eye shall see him*, and they also which pierced him; and all kindreds of the earth shall wail because of him."

Luke 21:26-27 — "...and then shall they see the Son of man coming in a cloud with power and great glory." His coming will be unexpected as a thief coming. "Behold, I come as a thief..." (Revelation 16:15).

II Peter 3:10 — "But the day of the Lord will come as a thief in the night."

It will be like the days of Noah. Matthew 24:37-39 — "But as the days of Noah were, so shall also the coming of the Son of man be. For as in the days that were before the flood they were eating and drinking, marrying and giving in marriage, until the day that Noah entered into the ark. And knew not until the flood came, and took them all away; so shall also the coming of the Son of man be." The hosts of heaven will accompany Him.

Matthew 16:17 — "And Jesus answered and said unto him, Blessed art thou, Simon Barjona: for flesh and blood hath not revealed it unto thee, but my Father which is in heaven."

Mark 13:26-27 — "And then shall they see the Son of man coming in the clouds with great power and glory. And then shall he send his angels, and shall gather together his elect from the four winds, from the uttermost parts of the earth to the uttermost part of heaven."

II Thessalonians 1:7 — "And to you who are troubled, rest with us, when the Lord Jesus shall be revealed from heaven with his mighty angels."

Five Things Will Take Place When Jesus Comes Again

1. The universal (all) resurrection of the dead
2. The rapture, or the righteous caught up to meet the Lord in the air
3. The general (all) judgment — both the righteous and the wicked
4. The reward of the righteous and the punishment of the wicked
5. The utter destruction of the earth and the aerial and planetary heavens that surround the earth

Chapter 11

THE RESURRECTION OF THE DEAD

Revelation 1:7 — "Every eye shall see him, and they also which pierced him." This is very noteworthy. Even those who pierced Him, though they have been in their graves hundreds of years, are going to rise. They will see Him again. This shows that both classes of the human family will be raised at the time he comes.

In Revelation 20:11–15 we see *all the dead* coming forth from land and sea, and immediately following are the judgment and the separation of the righteous and the wicked. "And I saw a great white throne, and him that sat on it, from whose face the earth and the heaven fled away; and there was found no place for them. And I saw the dead, small and great, stand before God; and the books were opened: and another book was opened, which is the book of life; and the dead were judged out of those things which were written in the books, according to their works.

And the sea gave up the dead which were in it; and death and hell delivered up the dead which were in them: and they were judged every man according to their works. And death and hell were cast into the lake of fire. This is the second death. And whosoever was not found written in the book of life was cast into the lake of fire."

I Corinthians 15:51–52 — "Behold, I show you a mystery; we shall not all sleep, but we shall *all be changed,* in a moment, in the twinkling of an eye, at the last trump: for the trumpet shall sound, and the dead shall be raised incorruptible, and we shall be changed." How many trumps can there be after the *last* trump? Here *all* the dead are call forth.

Now let us hear the words of Jesus in John 5:28-29 — "For the hour is coming, in the which *all that are in the graves* shall hear his voice, and shall come forth; they that have done good, unto the resurrection of life; and they that have done evil, unto the resurrection of damnation." No thousand years between here. And Paul told Felix, "That there shall be *a resurrection* of the dead, both of the just and unjust." If there were to be two resurrections he would have said, "There shall be two resurrections of the dead, one of the just, and the other of the unjust."

Philippians 3:20-21 — "For our conversation is in heaven; from whence also we look for the Saviour, the Lord Jesus Christ: Who shall change our vile body, that it may be fashioned like unto his glorious body, according to the working whereby he is able even to subdue all things unto himself."

I Corinthians 15:42-44 — "So also is the resurrection of the dead. It is sown in corruption; it is raised in incorruption: It is sown in dishonor; it is raised in glory: it is sown in weakness; it is raised in power: It is sown a natural body; it is raised a spiritual body. There is a natural body, and there is a spiritual body."

Let us not confuse this general resurrection of the dead with the first resurrection from being dead in our sins. Ephesians 5:14 — "Awake thou that sleepest, and arise from the dead, and Christ shall give thee light."

John 10:10 — "I am come that they might have life."

John 5:24–25 — "Verily, verily, I say unto you. He that heareth my word, and believeth on him that sent me, hath everlasting life, and shall not come into condemnation: but is *passed from death unto life*. Verily, verily, I say unto you. The hour is coming and now is when the dead shall hear the voice of the Son of God: and they that hear shall live." The first resurrection is spiritual.

Ephesians 2:1, 5–6 — "You hath he quickened [made alive] who were dead in trespasses and sins. Even when we were dead in sins, hath quickened us together with Christ, (by grace ye are saved;) And hath raised us up together and made us sit together in heavenly places in Christ Jesus."

Colossians 2:12–13 — "Buried with him in baptism, wherein also ye are risen with him through the faith of the operation of God, who hath raised him from the dead. And you, being dead in your sins and the uncircumcision of your flesh, hath he quickened together with him, having forgiven you all trespasses."

The Kingdom Delivered Up, the Righteous Caught Up

First Thessalonians 4:13-17 — "But I would not have you to be ignorant, brethren, concerning them which are asleep, that ye sorrow not, even as others which have no hope. For if we believe that Jesus died and rose again, even so them also which sleep in Jesus will God bring with him. For this we say unto you by the word of the Lord, that we which are alive and remain unto the coming of the Lord shall not prevent them which are asleep. For the Lord himself shall descend from heaven with a shout, with the voice of the archangel, and with the trump of God: and the dead in Christ shall rise first: Then we which are alive and remain shall be caught up together with them in the clouds, to meet the Lord in the air, and so shall we ever be with the Lord." Here the apostle is writing exclusively on the future hope of the church. The wicked are not being considered. The dead in Christ will be raised first, then we the living who are left over shall at the same time with them be caught away in the clouds for a meeting of the Lord in the air.

Paul, we said, had a hope toward God that there would be a resurrection of the dead, both of the just and unjust. Acts 24:15 — "And have hope toward God, which they themselves also allow, that there shall be a resurrection of the dead, both of the just and unjust." And Jesus spoke of all that are in the graves hearing his voice and coming forth. John 5:28 — "Marvel not at this: for the hour is coming, in the which all that are in the graves shall hear his voice." Surely one cannot find in the scriptures we've read the Lord coming and secretly taking the saved up to glory and the rest not finding it out until later.

Chapter 12

THE GENERAL JUDGMENT

Second Timothy 4:1 — "The Lord Jesus Christ, who shall judge the quick [living] and the dead at his appearing and his kingdom." Instead of the Lord setting up a thousand-year reign on the earth when he returns in his second advent and at a later time judging the wicked, he will judge the quick and the dead (who are raised from their graves) *at this appearing.* "And his kingdom" means *the righteous will enter his eternal kingdom of glory in heaven.* Paul said he delivers up the kingdom to the Father.

Romans 14:10–12 — ". . . So then every one of us shall give account of himself to God."

II Corinthians 5:10–11 — "For we must *all appear* before the judgment seat of Christ; that every one may receive the things done in his body, according to that he hath done, whether it be good or bad." In Ecclesiastes 12:14 we read, "For God shall bring every work into judgment, with every secret thing, whether it be good, or whether it be evil."

Revelation 22:12, 14, 15 — "And, behold, I come quickly: and my reward is with me, to give every man according as his work shall be. Blessed are they that do his commandments, that they may have right to the tree of life, and may enter in through the gates into the city. For without are dogs, and sorcerers, and whoremongers, and murderers, and idolaters, and whosoever loveth and maketh a lie."

Matthew 25:31–41 — "When the Son of man shall come in his glory, and all the holy angels with him, then shall he sit upon the throne of his glory: and before him shall be gathered all nations: and he shall separate them one from another, as a shepherd divideth his sheep from the goats: And he shall set the sheep on his right hand, but the goats on the left. Then shall the King say unto them on his right hand, Come, ye blessed of my Father, inherit the kingdom prepared for you from the foundation of the world: For I was ahungered, and ye gave me meat; I was thirsty, and ye gave me drink; I was a stranger, and ye took me in; Naked, and ye clothed me; I was sick, and ye visited me; I was in prison, and ye came unto me. Then shall the righteous answer him, saying, Lord, when saw we thee ahungered, and fed thee? or thirsty and gave thee drink? When saw we thee a stranger, and took thee in? or naked, and clothed thee? Or when saw we thee sick, or in prison, and came unto thee? And the King shall answer and say unto them, Verily I say unto you, Inasmuch as ye have done it unto one of the least of these my brethren, ye have done it unto me. Then shall he say also unto them on the left hand, Depart from me, ye cursed, into everlasting fire, prepared for the devil and his angels." This passage refers to an universal judgment of all men, good and bad, at the *second,* or *next coming* of Christ.

In Matthew 13:30, 39-40, 43 is Jesus' account of the wheat and the tares: "Let both grow together until the harvest; and in the time of harvest I will say to the reapers. Gather ye together first the tares, and bind them in bundles to burn them; but gather the wheat into my barn. The enemy that sowed them is the devil; the harvest is the end of the world; and the reapers are the angels. As therefore the tares are gathered and burned in the fire: so shall it be in the end of this world. Then shall the righteous shine forth as the sun in the kingdom of their Father. Who hath ears to hear, let him hear." The harvest is the end of the world. Both are judged. The tares are dealt with first. In Matthew 24:40 Jesus says, "One shall be taken, and the other left." Who is taken first? Not the saint, but the sinner.

In II Thessalonians 1:7–10 we read, ". . . who shall be punished with everlasting destruction from the presence of the Lord, and from the glory of his power: *when he shall come to be glorified in his saints.*" Here we find that the wicked are punished and Christ is glorified in his saints at the very instant when he comes the next time.

Chapter 13

THE REWARDS AND PUNISHMENT

Matthew 25:31–46 — "When the Son of man shall come in his glory, and all the holy angels with him, then shall he sit upon the throne of his glory: and before him shall be gathered all nations: and he shall separate them one from another, as a shepherd divideth his sheep from the goats: And he shall set the sheep on his right hand, but the goats on the left. Then shall the King say unto them on his right hand, Come, ye blessed of my Father, inherit the kingdom prepared for you from the foundation of the world: For I was ahungered, and ye gave me meat; I was thirsty, and ye gave me drink; I was a stranger, and ye took me in; Naked, and ye clothed me; I was sick, and ye visited me; I was in prison, and ye came unto me. Then shall the righteous answer him, saying, Lord, when saw we thee ahungered, and fed thee? or thirsty and gave thee drink? When saw we thee a stranger, and took thee in? or naked, and clothed thee? Or when saw we thee sick, or in prison, and came unto thee? And the King shall answer and say unto them, Verily I say unto you, Inasmuch as ye have done it unto one of the least of these my brethren, ye have done it unto me. Then shall he say also unto them on the left hand, Depart from me, ye cursed, into everlasting fire, prepared for the devil and his angels: For I was ahungered, and ye gave me not meat; I was thirsty, and ye gave me not drink; I was a stranger, and ye took me not in: naked, and ye clothed me not; sick, and in prison, and ye visited me not. Then shall they also answer him, saying, Lord, when saw we thee ahungered, or athirst, or a stranger, or naked, or sick, or in prison, and did not minister unto thee? Then shall he answer them, saying, Verily I say unto you, Inasmuch as ye did it not to one of the least of these, ye did it not to me. And these shall go away into everlasting punishment: but the righteous into life eternal."

Matthew 16:27 — "For the Son of man shall come in the glory of his Father with his angels and then he shall reward every man according to his works."

Revelation 22:11–12 — "Behold, I come quickly; *and my reward is with me,* to give every man according as his work shall be."

Jude 14-15 — "And Enoch also, the seventh from Adam, prophesied of these saying, Behold the Lord cometh with the thousands of his saints, to execute judgment upon all and to convince all that are ungodly among them of all their ungodly deeds which they have ungodly committed, and of all their hard speeches which ungodly sinners have spoken against him."

Revelation 11:18 — "And the nations were angry, and thy wrath is come, and the time of the dead, that they should be judged, and that thou shouldest give reward unto thy servants the prophets, and to the saints, and them that fear thy name, small and great: and shouldest destroy them which destroy the earth."

Chapter 14

THE UTTER DESTRUCTION OF THE EARTH

Psalm 102:25–26 — "Of old hast thou laid the foundation of the earth: and the heavens are the work of thy hands. They shall perish, but thou shalt endure; yea, all of them shall wax old like a garment; as a vesture shalt thou change them, and they shall be changed." These verses tell us that the heavens and the earth shall perish.

Isaiah 24:19–20 — "The earth is utterly broken down, the earth is clean dissolved, the earth is moved exceedingly. The earth shall reel to and fro like a drunkard, and shall be removed like a cottage: and the transgression thereof shall be heavy upon it: and it shall fall, and not rise again."

Isaiah 51:6 — "Lift up your eyes to the heavens, and look upon the earth beneath: for the heavens shall vanish away like smoke, and the earth shall wax old like a garment, and they that dwell therein shall die in like manner: but my salvation shall be for ever, and my righteousness shall not be abolished." Jesus said in the Sermon on the Mount, "Till heaven and earth pass."

Peter in II Peter 3:7–15 tells us of the "day of the Lord" (Christ's next coming) and that the earth shall be burned up (not burned over and purified) and the heavens around the earth shall pass away. "But the heavens and the earth, which are now, by the same word are kept in store, reserved unto fire against the day of judgment and perdition of ungodly men. But, beloved, be not ignorant of this one thing, that one day is with the Lord as a thousand years, and a thousand years as one day. The Lord is not slack concerning his promise, as some men count slackness: but is long-suffering to us-ward, not willing that any should perish, but that all should come to repentance. But the day of the Lord will come as a thief in the night: in the which the heavens shall pass away with a great noise, and the elements shall melt with fervent heat, the earth also and the works that are therein shall be burned up. Seeing then that all these things shall be dissolved, what manner of person ought ye to be in all holy conversation and godliness. Looking or and hasting unto the coming of the day of God, wherein the heavens being on fire shall be dissolved, and the elements shall melt with fervent heat? Nevertheless we, according to his promise, look for new heavens and a new earth, wherein dwelleth righteousness. Wherefore, beloved, seeing that ye look for such things, be diligent that ye may be found of him in peace, without spot, and blameless. And account that in the long-suffering of our Lord is salvation; even as our beloved brother Paul also according to the wisdom given unto him hath written unto you."

The Scriptures very clearly teach that Christ will come in the end of the world. They also inform us that this last day will be the day of judgment. And here Peter tells us plainly that on that very day of His coming and the judgment, the heavens and the earth will be consumed, melted, and destroyed. So this time will indeed be the end of the world, the close of all time allotted to this earth. All Scriptures teach that we are living in the last dispensation of time; that "now" is the day of salvation, that at the second advent of Christ He will not set up a kingdom, but will deliver up the kingdom to the Father.

We see from the above plain Scriptures that there will be *no time* and *no place* for a future millennial reign of Christ. Second Timothy 4:1 says Christ "shall judge the quick and the dead at his appearing and his kingdom." Paul said, "We must through much tribulation enter the kingdom of God." Peter said, "For so an entrance shall be ministered unto you abundantly into the everlasting kingdom of our Lord and Saviour Jesus Christ." "Come, ye blessed of my Father, inherit the kingdom prepared for you from the foundation of the world" (Matthew 25:34).

THE TRUE ISRAEL OF GOD

Chapter 15

WILL THERE BE A MILLENNIUM?

The term *millennium* means the space of 1,000 years. It usually implies that Christ will reign on this earth for 1,000 years, based largely on the 20th chapter of Revelation.

The word *millennium* is not found in the Bible.

What is the basic doctrine of premillennialism? Lawrence Chesnut very ably sets forth the doctrine, as follows, in his book *Will There Be a Millennium?*, pages 18 and 19:

1. **A political kingdom** — the premillennial theory holds that the kingdom of God is yet future and that it will be a political kingdom to be set up by Christ at His return.

A. Christ is to be a political king. Christ is to sit upon the throne of David and rule with a rod of iron over all nations of earth. He is to be King of kings and Lord of lords. All nations are to serve and obey him. All kings, ministers, presidents, governors, mayors, and all other officers will receive their appointments from Him.

B. The Jewish kingdom is to be restored. The restored Jewish kingdom, with Christ as king, will be the center of earthly rule. The tribes of Israel will return to Palestine and accept Christ as their Messiah. They are to be a favored nation. Christ will rule with Jerusalem as His Capital, and his twelve apostles will rule over the twelve tribes.

2. The restoration of Judaism — the Jewish religion is to be restored in the millennium.

A. The Temple is to be rebuilt. The temple is to be built in Jerusalem and will be more glorious than the Temple of Solomon, or the Temple of Herod. Temple worship will be restored. People all over the world will come to Jerusalem annually to worship.

B. Jewish laws and ritual will be in force. Circumcision and the Sabbath will be observed. Mosaic laws of marriage and divorce will apply, hence there will be marriage and death in the millennium.

C. Jewish ritual will be restored. The sons of Zadok are to be priests. They are to offer animal sacrifices, including sin offerings. This would mean the blood of Christ will no longer be efficacious for sin.

3. Order of events ushering in the millennium:

A. Christ will come secretly, as a thief in the night, to steal away his bride. First the righteous dead will be resurrected, then accompanied by the living righteous; they will be caught away for the rapture in the skies for a period usually said to be seven years. Those left behind will not know when this happens until they discover that their friends are missing.

B. The great tribulation then occurs. Seven years of the worst tribulation the world has ever known will trouble the earth during the absence of the saints. The antichrist will exercise his power during this period.

C. The appearance of Christ then follows. Christ returns from the rapture with great demonstration and *sets up His kingdom*. The devil is bound, and there follow a thousand years of peaceful reign on the earth. There will be ease and plenty for all.

D. The final judgment follows. At the close of the millennial reign the wicked will be resurrected. Satan will be loosed for a little season and will lead a great rebellion, which Christ will put down with much bloodshed. Then follows the final judgment, when Satan and the antichrist will be destroyed.

Let's look at that 20th chapter of Revelation:

1. It does not mention Christ's second coming.
2. It does not mention a bodily resurrection. John saw the "souls" (verse 4).
3. It does not mention a reign on earth; it is with Christ in paradise.
4. It does not mention Christ as being on earth.
5. It does not mention us.
6. The reign of the martyrs in verse 4 took place with Christ, in paradise, during the thousand years of the reign of the "beast" during the dark ages. Keep in mind these were disembodied spirits that were reigning with Christ.

The promises of the millennial theory are not spiritual, but sensual. The millennium does not promise a better of experience of salvation than is now obtainable. It does not promise to make men holier than they are now, nor can it offer better terms of grace. It holds no promises of spiritual blessing in advance of what saved men now possess.

To identify the red dragon of Revelation 20, we have to turn back to the 12th chapter of Revelation, verses 1–11 — "And there appeared a great wonder in heaven: a woman clothed with the sun, and the moon under her feet, and upon her head a crown of twelve stars: And she being with child cried, travailing in birth, and pained to be delivered. And there appeared another wonder in heaven; and behold a great red dragon, having seven heads and ten horns, and seven crowns upon his heads. And his tail drew the third part of the stars of heaven, and did cast them to the earth: and the dragon stood before the woman which was ready to be delivered, for to devour her child as soon as it was born. And she brought forth a man child, who was to rule all nations with a rod of iron: and her child was caught up unto God, and to his throne. And the woman fled into the wilderness, where she hath a place prepared of God, that they should feed her there a thousand two hundred and threescore days. And there was war in heaven: Michael and his angels fought against the dragon: and the dragon fought and his angels, and prevailed not; neither was their place found any more in heaven. And the great dragon was cast out, that old serpent, called the Devil, and Satan, which deceiveth the whole world, he was cast out into the earth, and his angels were cast out with him. And I heard a loud voice saying in heaven, Now is come salvation, and strength, and the kingdom of our God, and the power of his Christ: for the accuser of our brethren is cast down, which accused them before our God day and night. And they overcame him by the blood of the Lamb, and by the word of their testimony; and they loved not their lives unto the death."

The Woman — the beautiful church of God as originally constituted in the morning time.

The Man Child — Everything reproduces "after his kind," so if God's church reproduces anything, it will be *more church*, or converts to Christ.

The true church of Christ exists in two great parts — the one represented by the woman continues on earth; the other, represented by the man child, is cut off from the earth through martyrdom and ascends to God above.

Isaiah 66:7-8 — "Before she travailed, she brought forth; before her pain came, she was delivered of a man child. Who hath heard such a thing? Who hath seen such things? Shall the earth be made to bring forth in one day? or shall a nation be born at once? for as soon as Zion travailed, she brought forth her children."

Ephesians 2:15 — "Having abolished in his flesh the enmity, even the law of commandments contained in ordinances: for to make in himself of twain one new man, so making peace."

The dragon (not the origin of Beelzebub in the world) was in the same "heaven" as the woman, not the heaven of heavens, but in the planetary heaven. And besides, the prince of darkness does not have seven heads and ten horns.

This scene is laid *this side of the cross* in the Christian dispensation for they overcame him (verse 11) *by the blood of the Lamb,* and by *the word of their testimony."* He was "called" the Devil and Satan because he was for a time successfully doing the devil's work.

This dragon (here called a great red dragon) is in Revelation 20 called *the* dragon, which shows that he has already been identified in Chapter 12. He represents a great political power. In Revelation the animal world is used to symbolize political things and humans to symbolize religious things.

Revelation 13:2 — "The dragon gave him (beast) his power, and his seat, and great authority." In a later parallel series (Chapter 17) an angel explains about the seven heads and ten horns. Verse 12 — "I will tell thee the mystery of . . . the beast . . . which hath the seven heads and ten horns. Of the heads, there are seven kings: five are fallen, and one is, and the other is not yet come. And the ten horns which thou sawest are ten kings, which have received no kingdom as yet." What was the great political power ruling the world when the church was first established? The *Roman Empire*. The dragon was the *pagan* Roman Empire which was then ruling under its sixth head, the Imperial — the Caesars.

The ten horns were explained as kingdoms yet to come (not in a future millennium). These were the ten minor kingdoms which grew up out of the Roman Empire during its decline and fall. They are generally enumerated by historians as Anglo-Saxons, Burundians, Franks, Huns, Heruli, Lombards, Ostrogoths, Suevi, Vandals, and Visigoths. It is evident that we have here the forces of *paganism* enthroned in and upheld by the Roman state, warring against the true church of God.

Spirits cannot be bound with chains. Satan is a spirit and cannot be bound with a literal chain. If he could, where would the chain be fastened? It definitely has a spiritual meaning. This great chain is symbolic of the great chain of the truth of God, symbolizing the great power of the Word of God.

Matthew 16:19 — "And I will give unto thee the keys of the kingdom of heaven: and whatsoever thou shalt bind on earth shall be bound in heaven; and whatsoever thou shalt loose on earth shall be loosed in heaven."

Romans 1:16 — "For I am not ashamed of the gospel of Christ: for it is the power of God unto salvation to every one that believeth: to the Jew first, and also to the Greek."

We note now in verses 4 and 6 of Revelation 20 that it was the souls of them that were *beheaded* for the witness of Jesus that reigned with Christ. These were disembodied spirits that had had part *in the first resurrection* (a spiritual resurrection). This *first resurrection* is not a literal one but is a resurrection by the power of God from a dead state in sin to life in Jesus Christ.

Let us see what the Scripture has to say about this first resurrection. Since, as we will see later, the final and universal resurrection of all the dead will take place at the instant of Christ's second advent, it follows conclusively that the first resurrection must precede his coming. But there can be no resurrection except there first be a death. Every unregenerated person is "dead in trespasses and sins."

Ephesians 2:1 — "And you hath he quickened, who were dead in trespasses and sins." And verse 5, "Even when we were dead in sins, hath quickened us together with Christ, (by grace are ye saved)." Before conversion we were dead in sin.

Colossians 2:13 — "And you, being dead in your sins and the uncircumcision of your flesh, hath he quickened together with him, having forgiven you all trespasses."

Romans 8:6 — "For to be carnally minded is death; but to be spiritually minded is life and peace."

First Timothy 5:6 — "But she that liveth in pleasure is dead while she liveth."

James 1:15 — "Then when lust hath conceived, it bringeth forth sin: and sin, when it is finished, bringeth forth death."

Romans 7:9 — "For I was alive without the law once, but when the commandment came, sin revived, and I died."

First John 3:14 — "We know that we have passed from death unto life, because we love the brethren. He that loveth not his brother abideth in death."

Ezekiel 18:4 — "Behold, all souls are mine: as the soul of the father, so also the soul of the son is mine: the soul that sinneth, it shall die."

Jesus said, "I am come that *they might have life,* and that they might have it more abundantly."

John 11:25–26 — "I am the resurrection and the life: he that believeth in me *though he were dead,* yet shall he live: and whosoever liveth and believeth in me shall never die."

Ephesians 5:14 — "Awake thou that sleepest, and arise from the dead, and Christ shall give thee light."

Could anything be plainer than John 5:24–25 — "Verily, verily, I say unto you, He that heareth my word and believeth on him that sent me, hath everlasting life, and shall not come into condemnation; but *is passed from death unto life.* Verily, verily,

I say unto you, the hour is coming, *and now is,* when the dead [spiritually dead] shall hear the voice of the Son of God, and *they that hear shall live.*" The first resurrection is spiritual; it is personal, conditional, and operative throughout the gospel age.

Paul exhorted the Roman brethren, "Yield yourselves unto God, as those *that are alive from the dead*" (Romans 6:13).

Ephesians 2:1, 5, 6 — "And you hath he quickened, who were dead in trespasses and sins. Even when we were dead in sins, hath quickened us together with Christ, (by grace ye are saved;) And hath raised us up together, and made us sit together in heavenly places in Christ Jesus."

Colossians 2:13 — "And you, being dead in your sins and the uncircumcision of your flesh, hath he quickened together with him, having forgiven you all trespasses."

Colossians 3:1 — "If ye then be risen with Christ, seek those things which are above, where Christ sitteth on the right hand of God."

These souls in verse 4 had taken part in the spiritual resurrection while they were on earth and were blessed and holy. Because of their trueness to God they "were beheaded for the witness of Jesus" after which they ascended into paradise, where we see them reigning with Christ. Not a word is said about people being literally resurrected and reigning on the earth. This reign was before the resurrection of the literal dead, for the resurrection of these does not take place until after the one thousand years and includes both good and bad.

Revelation 20:11–15 — "And I saw a great white throne, and him that sat on it, from whose face the earth and the heavens fled away: and there was found no place for them. And I saw the dead, small and great, stand before God: and the books were opened: and another book was opened, which is the book of life: and the dead were judged out of those things which were written in the books, according to their works. And the sea gave up the dead which were in it: and death and hell delivered up the dead which were in them: and they were judged every man according to their works. And death and hell were cast into the lake of fire. This is the second death. And whosoever was not found written in the book of life was cast into the lake of fire." There is only *one future coming of our Lord,* and only *one future resurrection*.

Matthew 24:31 — "What shall be the sign of thy coming?"

Mark 13:26 — "And then shall they see the Son of man coming in the clouds with great power and glory."

I Corinthians 1:7 — ". . . waiting for *the coming* of our Lord Jesus Christ."

First Corinthians 15:23 — "But every man in his own order: Christ the first fruits: afterward they that are Christ's at his coming."

I Thessalonians 5:23 — "And the very God of peace sanctify you wholly: and I pray God your whole spirit and soul and body be preserved blameless unto the coming of our Lord Jesus Christ."

James 5:8 — "Be ye also patient: stablish your hearts; for the coming of the Lord draweth nigh."

Hebrews 9:28 — "So Christ was once offered to bear the sins of many; and unto them that look for him shall he appear the second time without sin unto salvation."

Second Timothy 4:8 — "Henceforth there is laid up for me a crown of righteousness, which the Lord, the righteous judge, shall give me at that day: and not to me only, but unto all them also that love his appearing."

Acts 24:15 — "And have hope toward God, which they themselves also allow, that there shall be a resurrection of the dead, both of the just and unjust."

Matthew 22:30 — "For in the resurrection they neither marry, nor are given in marriage, but are as the angels of God in heaven."

Romans 6:5 — "For if we have been planted together in the likeness of his death, we shall be also in the likeness of his resurrection."

Philippians 3:11 — "If by any means I might attain unto the resurrection of the dead."

Chapter 16

THERE IS A FORM OF GODLINESS

I have been known down through the years as a very optimistic person; however, I am also a realist, and when God's eternal "Word" tells me in II Timothy 3:1–5 that "in the last days perilous times shall come, for men shall be lovers of their own selves, covetous, boasters, proud, blasphemers, disobedient to parents, unthankful, unholy, without natural affection, truce breakers, false accusers, incontinent, fierce, despisers of those that are good, traitors, heady, high-minded, lovers of pleasure more than lovers of God, *having a form of godliness,* but denying the power thereof; from such turn away," I must believe this.

In II Timothy 4:1 we read, "Now the Spirit speaketh expressly, that in the latter times some shall depart from the faith, giving heed to seducing spirits, and doctrines of devils; speaking lies in hypocrisy; having their conscience seared with a hot iron."

We could use many more Scriptures, and I do want to ask you to look at Revelation 2:1–5 — "Unto the angel of the church of Ephesus write: These things saith he that holdeth the seven stars in his right hand, who walketh in the midst of the seven golden candlesticks; I know thy works, and thy labor, and thy patience, and how thou canst not bear them which are evil; and thou hast tried them which say they are apostles, and are not, and hast found them liars. And hast borne, and hast patience, and for my name's sake hast labored, and hast not fainted. Nevertheless I have somewhat against thee, because thou has left thy first love. Remember therefore from whence thou art fallen, and repent, and do the first works; or else I will come unto thee quickly, and will remove thy candlestick out of his place, except thou repent."

This was a local church of God. This was a church that Paul labored to build and at one time was a powerful local church of God and then just a few years later she had lost everything that was worthwhile. I must ask, "How could it happen?" Today we are living in a time when many local churches have grown cold in their relationship with God. If God was writing about your church in the manner He did about the seven churches of Asia, I wonder just what He would write. It would be interesting to know.

In I Peter 3:12 we read, "For the eyes of the Lord are over the righteous, and His ears are open unto their prayers." *What a promise.* Consider with me the marvelous truths in Revelation 21:1-4 — "And I saw a new heaven and a new earth: for the first heaven and the first earth were passed away: and there was no more sea. And I John saw the holy city, new Jerusalem, coming down from God out of heaven, prepared as a bride adorned for her husband. And I heard a great voice out of heaven saying, Behold, the tabernacle of God is with men, and he will dwell with them, and they shall be his people, and God himself shall be with them and be their God. And God shall wipe away all tears from their eyes: and there shall be no more death, neither sorrow, nor crying, neither shall there be any more pain: for the former things are passed away." Remember, this is *forever*. I want you to be there. There is nothing that this "old world" has to offer that can compare with that which my heavenly Father says He will give you: "I have prepared for you." In Revelation 22:1–7 we have these words, "And he showed me a pure river of water of life, clear as crystal, proceeding out of the throne of God and of the Lamb. In the midst of the street of it, and on either side of the river, was there the tree of life, which bare twelve manner of fruits, and yielded her fruit every month: and the leaves of the tree were for the healing of the nations. And there shall be no more curse: but the throne of God and of the Lamb shall be in it: and his servants shall serve him: And they shall see his face; and his name shall be on their foreheads. And there shall be no night there; and they need no candle, neither light of the sun: for the Lord God giveth them light; and they shall reign for ever and ever. And he said unto me, These sayings are faithful and true: and the Lord God of the holy prophets sent his angel to show unto his servants the things which must shortly be done. Behold, I come quickly: blessed is he that keepeth the sayings of the prophecy of this book." And in verses 16 and 17, "I Jesus have sent mine angel to testify unto you these things in the churches. I am the root and the offspring of David, and the bright and morning star. And the Spirit and the bride say, Come. And let him that heareth say, Come. And let him that is athirst come. And whosoever will, let him take the water of life freely." Did you just hear the words of Jesus? "Let him that heareth *come*."

I would hope this song written by Fanny J. Crosby (1820–1915) under the anointing of the Holy Spirit will challenge you to live "Close to God." This is my prayer.

Thou, my everlasting portion. More than friend or life to me;

All along my pilgrim journey, Savior, let me walk with Thee.

Close to Thee, close to Thee, close to Thee, close to Thee;

All along my pilgrim journey, Savior, let me walk with Thee.

Not for ease or worldly pleasure, Nor for fame my prayer shall be;

Gladly will I toil and suffer, Only let me walk with Thee.

Close to Thee, close to Thee, close to Thee, close to Thee;

Gladly will I toil and suffer, Only let me walk with Thee.

Lead me through the vale of shadows. Bear me o'er life's fitful sea;

Then the gate of life eternal may I enter, Lord, with Thee.

Close to Thee, close to Thee, close to Thee, close to Thee;

Then the gate of life eternal may I enter, Lord, with Thee.

Epilogue

What a Tragedy!

Those of you who have wandered through the first four chapters of this book have found that the Jewish nation, as a whole, is looking for a Jewish Messiah. What a tragedy! Everything they have been looking for, wanting, expecting, and desiring can be found in the Messiah that hung on "the old rugged cross." That sad day of the world when He paid for our sins there. Jesus said, "If you have faith as a grain of mustard seed, you could say to yonder mountain be removed into the sea, and it would be done" (Matthew 17:20). How much faith will it take to "mow down" all the enemies that ever opposed the children of Israel? Let us be sure to bear in mind Jesus' teaching that a born-again Christian has already laid down his literal warfare and now he is dealing in spiritual warfare. This is the kind of warfare that Jesus says if we ask Him with faith as the grain of a mustard seed that He will "mow down" the enemy, the devil, and all his workings. Do we not read, "His eyes are over the righteous and ears are open unto their prayers"? (I Peter 3:12). Does not this plain New Testament teaching tell us, "If we abide in Him and His words abide in us, we shall ask what we will and it will be done"? (John 15:7). Surely a childlike simple faith in Christ can and will produce deliverance from every enemy of the world in a Jewish heart as well as meeting every need of a born-again Christian in one's life.

Oh, that the Jewish nation could only see this, certainly there would be a revival such as we have not seen before! My prayer is that they will see this.

BIBLIOGRAPHY

I Esdras
The Apocrypha, Oxford Press, Humphrey Milford
II Esdras
The Apocrypha, Oxford Press, Humphrey Milford
I Baruch
Charles, Volume One and Two
II Baruch
Charles, Volume One and Two
III Baruch
Charles, Volume One and Two
I Enoch
Charles, Volume One and Two
II Enoch
Charles, Volume One and Two
Ezekiel
The Old Testament
Sibylline Oracles
Charles, Volume One and Two
IV Ezra
Charles, Volume One and Two
Zechariah
The Old Testament
Revelation
The New Testament
Shepherd of Hermas
Lost Books of the Bible, Alpha House, Inc., Publisher
Lost Gospel of Peter
Lost Books of the Bible, Alpha House, Inc., Publisher

THE TRUE ISRAEL OF GOD